Selections from
The American State Papers
Monograph Numbers 5, 6, and 7

SPANISH AND BRITISH LAND GRANTS IN MISSISSIPPI TERRITORY 1750–1784

Clifford Neal Smith

CLEARFIELD

Monograph Numbers 5, 6, and 7
Copyright © 1996 by Westland Publications
All Rights Reserved.

Monograph Numbers 5, 6, and 7
Originally published
McNeal, Arizona, 1996

Reprinted, three parts in one volume, for
Clearfield Company, Inc. by
Genealogical Publishing Co., Inc.
Baltimore, Maryland
2004

International Standard Book Number: 0-8063-5241-8

Made in the United States of America

Selections from **The American State Papers**
Monograph Number 5

SPANISH AND BRITISH LAND GRANTS

IN MISSISSIPPI TERRITORY, 1750-1784

CLIFFORD NEAL SMITH

First printing, September 1996   rz

FOREWORD

The American State Papers are official public documents printed privately long before the Congressional Printing Office existed. The printing of public documents during the very early Congresses was done without any general provision of law as to what should be printed. Even as early as 1829 the clerk of the House of Representatives reported that, for the period 1793-1803 not a vestige of manuscript and only a scattered few printed copies were extant. A contributing factor was the destruction of the Capitol building in 1814 by fire.

In 1821 a bill was passed which authorized the publication of 750 copies of all the documents that could be found. The documents were published by two private companies: Gales and Seaton, and Duff Green. Of the two publications, Gales and Seaton is the larger. The Duff Green collection of documents are less comprehensive than the Gales and Seaton collection, and there are many differences in the pagination, particularly in later volumes.

Both publishers appear to have divided the original documents into general subject categories: Foreign Affairs, Indian Affairs, Finance, Commerce and Navigation, Military Affairs, Naval Affairs, Post Office Department, Public Land, and Claim. For genealogical and family history researchers, the last two categories--Public Land and Claims--are the most valuable, and it is from these two categories that this monograph *Selections from* ***The American State Papers*** will be made. The Public Land category, in eight volumes, covers the period 1789-1837; the Claims category, in one volume, covers the period 1790-1823.

In 1972 an attempt was made to index all names in the Public Land and Claims categories of the American State Papers; the index, although monumental, is, however, not complete. All researchers are urged to read pages i through xxvii of

Phillip McMullin, editor, *Grassroots of America: A Computerized Index to the American State Papers: Land Grants and Claims (1789-1837) with Other Aids to Research* (Salt Lake City, Utah: Gendex Corporation, 1972).

The present *Selections from the American State Papers* are the selections, by narrower subject matter, from the Gales and Seaton edition, made by this compiler for the use of genealogists and family historians because the original volumes are now very rare and, no doubt, inaccessible to most researchers.

(ASP 8:1:594)

[Document] 150, 10th Congress, 1st Session
Communicated to Congress, April 22, 1808

To the Senate and House of Representatives of the United States.

I transmit to both Houses of Congress a letter from the Envoy of His Britannic Majesty, at this place, to the Secretary of State, on the subject of certain British claims to land in the territory of Mississippi, relative to which several acts have been heretofore passed by the Legislature.

Th[omas] Jefferson

April 22, 1808

I have the honor to lay before the Government of the United States, by His Majesty's command, a copy of a memorial which has been presented by Mr. — **Canning**, His Majesty's principal Secretary of State for Foreign Affairs, by several British subjects, proprietors of lands in His Majesty's late province of West Florida.

As I have already had the honor of explaining to you the well founded claims which the memorialists have upon the justice and liberality of the United States, for some remedy against the effects of a certain act of Congress, which was passed on the 2d of March, 1805, entitled "An act further to amend an act entitled An act regulating the grants of land, and providing for the disposal of the lands of the United States, south of the State of Tennessee;" and as the enclosed memorial, and the documents accompanying it, most fully and clearly exhibit the injury which the provisions of that act occasion to their rights and equitable claims upon some of the lands in His Majesty's late province of West Florida therein comprehended.

I will, therefore, only beg leave to repeat my request that the Government of the United States will be pleased to pay a serious and early attention to these facts, now stated and laid before them, fully relying upon the known principles of equity and liberality which govern the conduct of nations in amity with each other, that some effectual relief will be afforded to the complainants by the timely intervention in their favor, by the Government of the United States.

I have the honor to be, sir, with very great respect, your most obedient, humble servant.

[signed] **D. M. Erskine**

[To] The Hon. **James Madison**, etc.

A.

To the Right Honorable Lord Hawkesbury, one of His Majesty's Principal Secretaries of State:

The memorial of the undersigned, proprietors of land in His Majesty's late province of West Florida, respectfully showeth:

That your memorialists have, with extreme surprise and mortification, recently received the printed paper annexed, purporting to be an act of the United States of America, in which the interests of your memorialists, and of many other British subjects in various parts of the world, are deeply involved.

That the said act effectually precludes your memorialists from the possibility of substantiating their claims after a very limited period, inasmuch as the 5th section thereof compels them to register their vouchers at *Natches, before the last day of March*, 1804.

That your memorialists will then be dispossessed of property which they had acquired by public services, by inheritance, or by purchase, in consequence of a provision, which, if it were practicable on their part, would expose them to the loss of their documents.

That the Legislature of America do not appear to have been fully aware of the injurious effect of the said section with respect to your memorialists; for it cannot be conceived they had it in contemplation without some imputed misconduct to deprive individuals of their property, in consequence of having obtained the sovereignty of the country.

Wherefore, your memorialists most earnestly entreat your lordship's interference in their behalf, humbly praying that you will take their case into consideration, and represent the fatal tendency of the said act, suggesting, as the means of affording the most compete redress, that the British records of West Florida, which have been delivered to the minister of the United States, should be adopted and acted upon as valid and decision in all cases whatsoever, and the rights of the various claimants established accordingly, or affording such other relief as your lordship, in your wisdom, shall deem adequate, and your memorialists, as in duty bound, will ever pray, etc.

Charles Shaw, for Major General -- **Stuart,**
Lieutenant General -- **Shaw,** and Major **John Shaw,**
Peter Swanson, for himself and the representatives of **John McGillivray**,
William Struthey,
James McGillivray, and **Charles Swede Stuart,**
J. Stephenson, for himself,
K. Lorimer,
Captain, -- **Gasling,**
Jonathan Ogden, and **John Bradley,**
W[illia]m Sulteney,
Archibald Dalzel,
Arthur Clarke,

John Miller,
William Ogilvy, for self and **John Falconer,**
Arthur Strother, for himself,
Thomas Strother,
James Amoss, and **Adam Amoss,**
John Miller, for Major **Alexander MacDonald,** and **Charles Roberts**
Peter Swanson, for the representatives of General -- **Johnston, R. A.,** and **William Godley,**
Edward Brocksopp, for himself and **John Frederick Bowrne.**

B.

Washington, March 31, 1804

My Lord:

I had the honor to receive, in the evening of the 22d instant, your lordship's separate despatches of the 9th of February, transmitting to me the copy of a memorial which you had received from several proprietors of lands in His Majesty's late province of West Florida, complaining of the injury which they are likely to sustain from the provisions of an act of the American Congress which passed in the course of their last session, and instructing me to lose no time in representing the circumstances of the case to the American Government, and to use every exertion of my power for the purpose of obtaining redress for those persons.

(ASP 8:1:595)

I accordingly delivered to Mr. -- **Madison** a representation on this subject, of which I have the honor to transmit a copy enclosed; accompanying it with a suggestion, that the President should give every possible weight to the object, by sending a message respecting it to the Congress. This measure proved, however, to be impracticable, from the circumstance of that body having agreed to rise on the 20th, whilst the Sunday which intervened rendered the time for business still shorter. All, then, that this Government could possibly do, as the Secretary of State has assured me, was to cause an amendment to take place, to the effect conceived to be desired by the British claimants, to a bill which was already pending before the Legislature, supplementary to the act in question passed in the last session.

Your lordship will find enclosed, together with a copy of Mr. -- **Madison**'s answer to me, an extract of the above mentioned supplementary act, by which you will perceive that the term for the admission of claims has been prolonged to the last day of November next, (the measure had been already proposed in the bill before my representation had been delivered,) and that the twelfth section, by providing for the admission as evidence of transcripts of the records of His Majesty's late province of West Florida, contains precisely what the British claimants stated in their memorial to your lordship would be the means of affording the most complete redress. At all events, the prolongation of the term now affords them an opportunity of seeing what further provisions may be necessary for securing to them their property and interests; which additional provisions may be made before the expiration of the new term given, because the Congress is to meet again on the first Monday in November, whilst, from the proof which the American Government have given on the present occasion, of their readiness to afford every assistance to the British claimants, there can be no doubt of their manifesting a similar friendly disposition on any further application which may be made to them.

It may be proper I should add, for the information of the persons concerned, that Mr. -- **Madison** acquainted me, yesterday, with his having just received notice of the arrival at Baltimore, from London, of the records above alluded to, and that he had given orders for the safe conveyance of them to his office.

> I have the honor to be, etc.
> [signed] **Ant[hony] Merry**

The Right Honorable Lord Hawkesbury, etc., etc.

To the Right Honorable **George Canning**, *one of His Majesty's principal Secretaries of State, the memorial of the undersigned, in behalf of themselves and other proprietors of lands in His Majesty's late province of West Florida, respectfully showeth:*

That, in consequence of a former memorial, of which a copy (A.) is annexed, instructions were transmitted to His Majesty's envoy, by a prompt application to the American Government, as appears by the correspondence, (B.) prevailed on them to repeal the obnoxious act, by passing an act supplementary, by which it is enacted, that "Transcripts of the records of the British province of West Florida, to claims for lands therein, and which have been delivered to the Government of the United States, may be produced as evidence, and shall be entitled to the same weight in any court of the United States as if the same had been delivered, or shall be delivered, either by the Registers of the Land Offices in the Mississippi territory, before the last of March, one thousand eight hundred and four, any thing in this act, or in the fifth section of the act to which this is a supplement, to the contrary notwithstanding."

That your memorialists, firmly believing their claims to have been thus incontrovertibly and definitely established, reposed in perfect security, under the persuasion that their lands would forever remain protected by the above recited act, till a fit opportunity should occur of settling or disposing of them.

That your memorialists, while they conceived their property to be thus completely protected, have recently been alarmed by a new act of Congress, (which they have just received from America, and of which a copy (C.) is annexed,) dated 2d March 1805, by which the holders of lands under British grants are entirely divested of such property, without resource, the time therein allowed for fulfilling the required conditions have already elapsed.

Under these circumstances, your memorialists earnestly entreat that some speedy and effectual remedy may be applied for their relief, either by an application for the repeal of the said act, or by obtaining a just compensation. And your memorialists, etc.

London, December 15, 1807.

Archibald Dalzel
Thomas Comyn,
James Jefferson, agent for the representatives of Major General -- **Small,**
J. Shearl, Major General,
George Varlo,
-- **Konovan,** for the Earl of Moira,
Charles Stuart
C. Brocksopp, for the honorable General -- **Harcourt,**
George Frere,
Arthur Clarke,
James Amoss,
Henry Goldfinch,
John Page, for the Admiral **John Ferguson**
William Garnier
Ar. Struther, for self and **John Nunn, J. T. Neil, Eleanor Neil, Catherine Lorimer,**
-- **Montgomeril,**
Charles Shaw, for Lieut. General -- **Shaw,**
William Wingdam Falling,
Alexander McDonald,
Will. Charles Wells, for the heirs of **Robert Wells,**
Richard Taitt, agent for **David Taitt,**
Peter Swanson, for self and **John Miller,**
Peter Swanson, for **John McGillivrayers,*** (so spelled)
Peter Swanson, for **Charles Roberts,**
Thomas Comyn, for **Wm. McKennon,**
Charles Shaw, for Major **W. Chesta,** Captain -- **Paul,** R.N. and Sir **Broderick Chennery.**
   By desire signed, by letter to him, as chairman,
Adam Gordon, for Major General Sir **G. Prevost,** Bt.

[There are letters of transmittal, etc., which are not given herein. The signers of such letters of transmittal were **Anthony Merry** to Honorable **James Madison; Nathaniel Macon,** Speaker of the House of Representatives, to **A. Burr,** Vice President of the United States and President of the Senate, and approved by **Th[omas] Jefferson.**]

(ASP 8:1:597)
[Document] 151

10th Congress, 1st Session

Claim to Bounty Land for Military Service Rendered to the State of Virginia. Communicated to the House of Representatives, April 23, 1808. Mr. **Jeremiah Morrow**, from the Committee on the Public Lands, to whom was referred the petition of **William Biggs,** made the following report:

The petitioner states that he was a lieutenant in the regiment commanded by General **George Rogers Clark,** in the service of the State of Virginia, and, as such, was entitled, under an act of Assembly of the said State, to a share in the one hundred and fifty thousand acres of land granted by that State to the officers and soldiers of the said regiment, and reserved by Virginia for that purpose, in her cession of the Western territory to the United States. That, at the time the distribution of the lands was made, the petitioner was a prisoner to the Wabash Indians; his name was not inserted on the list among those entitled to a share; that, on his release from captivity, which he procured by the payment of a sum of money, he made application to the commissioners appointed to make distribution of the lands, for his proportional shares; but was informed that the whole of the land had been distributed among the other officers and soldiers.

He prays that two thousand acres of land (being the quantity he was entitled to,) be granted to him in the Illinois country, or adjoining the tract reserved for the officers and soldiers of the regiment.

The committee, on examining the subject, are of opinion that the petitioner has no just claim on the United States, arising out of any error injustice in the distribution of land reserved by the State of Virginia for a regiment of her State troops. The distribution was not made under the authority of the United States. The reserve was special, and it is not alleged that the quantity reserved has not been appropriated. The United States are bound by the act of cession faithfully to dispose of the residue of the lands to the general benefit of the Union; therefore, they are not at liberty to make gratuitous grants. The committee respectfully submit the following resolution:

Resolved, That the petition have leave to withdraw his petition.

[The land grants made to Virginia veterans of the Revolutionary War by the Commonwealth of Virginia are indexed in: Clifford Neal Smith, Federal Land Series, volume 4, parts 1 and 2. **William Biggs** is not listed therein, nor in any of the other volumes of the Series.]

(ASP 8:1:598)

[Documents 153 and 154 contain little of direct interest; one is a transmittal letter signed by **Albert Gallatin**, dated 2 January 1809. However, the "Conditions" to Document 154 are of relevance and are reproduced hereinafter. They are dated Mississippi Territory, Town of Washington, 3 July 1807, and are signed by the Board of Commissioners, **Thomas Rodney, Robert William,** and **Thomas H. Williams.**]

(ASP 8:1:599)

Conditions

1. Let a patent be prepared and engrossed, to pass the great seal of this province, importing His Majesty's most gracious grant unto **Captain Amos Ogden**, his heirs and assigns, of a plantation or tract of land, containing twenty-five thousand acres, situate southwesterly about twenty-one miles from the old Natchez fort, bounded southerly by a creek called Homochitta creek, and about one-quarter of a mile east of a tract of one thousand acres, granted to **Colin Graham, Esq.**, on said creek, about half a mile south from land granted to **James Hooper,** on a creek called Second creek, and on the other side of vacant land; together with all rights, members, privileges, and appurtenances to the same, being or in anywise belonging, upon the following terms, conditions, and reservations, viz.: That the said **Amos Ogden** do settle the said lands with foreign Protestants, or persons that shall be brought from His Majesty's other colonies in North America, within ten years from the date of the grant, in the proportion of one person for every hundred acres. That if one-third of the land is not settled with foreign Protestants, or persons that shall be brought from His Majesty's other colonies in North America, at the expiration of ten years from the date of the grant, do revert to His Majesty, his heirs, and successors. That an annual quit-rent of one halfpenny sterling per acre be reserved to His Majesty, his heirs, and successors, payable on the feast of St. Michael which shall first happen after the expiration of five years from the date of the grant, and to be payable on every ensuing feast of St. Michael, or within fourteen days after; and the whole quantity to be subject in like manner to the like quit-rents, at the expiration of ten years, which the surveyor shall, upon the return of survey, report to be proper for erecting fortifications, public wharfs, and naval years, or for other military purposes. That there be a reservation to His Majesty, his heirs, and successors, of all mines of gold, silver, copper, lead, and coals. That, if any part of the land shall appear, by the surveyor's report, to be well adapted to the growth of help or flax, it shall be a condition of the grant that the grantee shall sow, and continue annually to cultivate, a due proportion of the land, not less than one acre in every thousand, with the beneficial article of produce; the same terms, conditions, and reservations above mentioned being conformable to His Majesty's order in council to me directed, bearing date the thirteenth day of May, in the year of our Lord one thousand seven hundred and sixty-seven, and with the other usual clauses, reservations, provisions, restrictions, and limitations, as contained in His Majesty's instructions, and, for so doing, this shall be your sufficient warrant.

[See Clifford Neal Smith, *Federal Land Series: A Calendar of Archival Materials on the Land Patents Issued by the United States Government, with Subject, Tract, and Name Indexes.* Volume 1: 1788-1810 and Volume 3: 1810-1814 (Chicago: American Library Association, 1972, 1980). The information in these volumes relates to the time just after the U.S. Government took over Mississippi Territory. No doubt, some of the descendants of persons mentioned in the British grant above will be found.]

2. To have and to hold the said tract of land, and all and singular the premises hereby granted, with the appurtenances, unto the said **Daniel Clark**, his heirs, and assigns, forever, in free and common soccage, yielding and paying unto us, our heirs, and successors, or to the Receiver General of our quit-rents for the time being, or to such other officer as shall be appointed to receive the same, a quit-rent of one halfpenny sterling per acre, at the feast of St. Michael, every year; the first payment to commence on the said feast day of St. Michael which shall first happen after the expiration of ten years from the date hereof, or within fourteen days after the said feast, annually: Provided, always, and this present grant is upon condition, that the said **Daniel Clark**, his heirs, and assigns, shall and do, within three years after the expiration of the term of ten years aforesaid, for every fifty acres of plantable land hereby granted, clear and cultivate three acres, at least, in that part thereof which he or they shall judge most convenient and advantageous, or else do clear and drain three acres of swampy or sunken ground, or do drain three acres of marsh, if any such shall be contained therein; and shall further, within the time aforesaid, put and keep upon every fifty acres thereof, accounted barren, three neat cattle, and continue the same thereon, until three acres, for every fifty acres, be fully cleared and improved; and if it shall so happen that there be no part of the said tract of land fit for cultivation within the time aforesaid, without manuring and improving the same, if the said **Daniel Clark**, his heirs, and assigns, shall within three years after the expiration of the ten years, as aforesaid, erect on some part of the said tract of land one good dwelling-house, to contain at least twenty feet in length, and

(ASP 8:1:600)

sixteen in breadth, and put on his said land the like number of three neat cattle, as aforesaid, for every fifty acres therein contained; or otherwise, if any part of said tract of land shall be stony or rocky ground, not fit for culture or pasture, shall and do, within three years, as aforesaid, besides erecting the said house, begin to employ thereon, and continue to work, for three years, then next ensuing, in digging any stone quarry or mine, one good and able hand for every hundred acres thereof, it shall be accounted a sufficient cultivation and improvement: Provided, also, that every three acres which shall be cleared and worked, or cleared and drained, as aforesaid, shall further be accounted a sufficient seating, planting, cultivation, and improvement, to save forever from forfeiture fifty acres of land in any part of the tract hereby granted; and the said **Daniel Clark**, his heirs, and assigns, shall be at liberty to withdraw his or their stock, or to forbear working in any quarry or mine, in proportion to such cultivation and improvements, aforesaid, as shall be made upon the plantable lands, swampy, sunken grounds, or marshes therein contained: Provided, also, that this grant shall be duly registered in the Register's Office of this province, with six months from the date thereof; and, also, that a docket thereof shall be entered in the Auditor's Office within the same time, if any such establishment shall take place in this province:

Provided, always, that the said **Daniel Clark**, his heirs, or assigns, at any time hereafter, having seated, planted, cultivated, and improved the said tract, or any part thereof, according to the directions and conditions above mentioned, may make proof of such seating, planting, cultivation, and improvement, in the general court, or in the court of the county district or precinct where the said land lieth, and have such proof certified to the Register's Office, and there entered with the record of this grant, a copy of which, duly attested, shall be admitted on any trial to prove the seating and planting of said land: Provided, always, nevertheless, that, if the said **Daniel Clark**, his heirs, and assigns, do not in all things full comply with, and fulfil, the respective directions and conditions herein set forth, for the proper cultivation of the said land, within the time herein above limited for the completion thereof; or if the said **Daniel Clark**, his heirs or assigns, shall not pay to us, our heirs, and successors, or to the Receiver General of our quit-rents or to the proper officer appointed to receive the same, the said quit-rent of one halfpenny sterling per acre, on the said feast of St. Michael, or within fourteen days after, annually, for every acre contained in this grant, that then, and in either of these cases, respectively, the grant shall be void, any thing herein contained to the contrary notwithstanding; and the said lands, tenements, hereditaments, and premises hereby specified, and every part and parcel thereof, shall revert to us, our heirs, and successors, fully and absolutely, as if the same had never been granted.
[See the footnote to Number 1 above.]

3. To have and to hold the said tract of land, and all and singular the premises hereby granted, with the appurtenances, unto the said **Christopher Guice,** his heirs and assigns, forever, in free and common soccage, yielding and paying unto us, our heirs, and successors, or to the Receiver General of our quit-rents for the time being, or to such other officer as shall be appointed to receive the same quit-rent of one halfpenny per acre, at the feast of St. Michael, every year, the first payment to commence on the said feast of St. Michael which shall first happen after the expiration of two years from the date hereof, or within fourteen days after the feast, annually; Provided, always, and this grant is upon condition, nevertheless, that the said **Christopher Guice**, his heirs or assigns, shall and do, within three years after the date hereof, for every fifty acres of plantable land hereby granted, clear and cultivate three acres, at least, in that part thereof which he or they shall judge most convenient and advantageous, or else do clear and drain three acres of swampy or sunken ground, or do drain three acres of marsh, if any such shall be contained therein, and shall further, within the time aforesaid, put and keep upon every fifty acres thereof accounted barren, three neat cattle, and continue the same thereon, until three acres, for every fifty acres, be fully cleared and improved; and if it shall so happen that there be no part of said tract of land fit for present cultivation, without manuring and improving the same, if the said **Christopher Guice**, his heirs, or assigns, shall, with three years from the date hereof, erect on some part of the said tract of land one good dwelling-house, to contain at least twenty feet in length and sixteen feet in breadth, and put on his said land the like number of three neat cattle, as aforesaid, on every fifty acres, therein contained; or, otherwise, if any part of the said tract of land shall be stony or rocky ground, not fit for culture or pasture, shall and do, within three years, as aforesaid, besides erecting the said house, begin to employ thereon, and continue to work fourteen years then next ensuing, in digging any stone quarry or mine, one good and able hand for every hundred acres thereof, it shall be accounted a sufficient cultivation and improvement; Provided, also, that every three acres which shall be cleared and worked, or

cleared and drained, as aforesaid, shall further be accounted a sufficient seating, planting, cultivation, and improvement, to save forever from forfeiture fifty acres of land, in any part of the tract hereby granted; And the said **Christopher Guice**, his heirs and assigns, shall be at liberty to withdraw his or their stock, or to forbear working in any quarry or mine, in proportion to such cultivation and improvements aforesaid, as shall be made upon the plantable lands, swamps, sunken grounds, or marshes, therein: Provided, also that this grant shall be duly registered in the Register's Office of this province, within six months from the date thereof; and, also, that a docket thereof shall be entered in the Auditor's Office, within the same time, if such establishment shall take place in this province: Provided, always, that the said **Christopher Guice,** his heirs, and assigns, at any time hereafter having seated, planted, cultivated, and improved the said land, or any part thereof, according to the directions and conditions above mentioned, may make good of such seating, planting, cultivation, and improvement in the general court, or in the court of the county, district, or province where the said land lieth, and have such proof registered in the Register's Office, and there entered with the record of this grant, a copy of which, duly attested, shall be admitted on trial, to prove the seating and planting of the said land: Provided, always nevertheless, that if the said **Christopher Guice**, his heirs and assigns, do not in all things fully comply with and fulfil the respective directions and conditions herein above set forth, for the proper cultivation of the said lands, within the time herein above limited for the completion thereof, or if the said **Christopher Guice**, his heirs, and assigns, shall not pay to us, our heirs, and successors, or to the Receiver General of our quit-rents, or to the proper officer appointed to receive the same, the said quit-rent of one halfpenny sterling per acre, on the said feast of St. Michael, or within fourteen days after, annually, for every acre contained in the grant; that, then, and in either of these cases, respectively, this grant shall be void, any thing contained herein to the contrary notwithstanding; and the said lands, tenements, hereditaments, and premises hereby specified, and every part and parcel thereof, shall revert to us, our heirs, and successors, fully and absolutely, as if the same had never been granted.

4. To have and to hold the said tract of land, and all and singular the premises being granted, with the appurtenances, unto the said **William Bay**, his heirs, and assigns, forever, in free and common soccage, yielding and paying unto us, our heirs, and successors, or to the Receiver General of our quit-rents for the time being, or to such other officer as shall be appointed to receive the same, a quit-rent of one halfpenny sterling per acre, at the feast of St. Michael every year; the first payment to commence on the said feast of St. Michael which shall first happen after the expiration of ten years from the date hereof, or with fourteen days after the said feast, annually. Provided, always, and this present grant is upon condition, nevertheless, that this grant shall be duly registered in the Register's Office of this province, within six months from the date hereof; and, also, that a docket thereof shall be entered in the Auditor's Office, within the same time, if such establishment shall take place in this province; And provided, also, that if the said **William Bay**, his heirs, and assigns, do not in all things fully comply with and fulfil the conditions herein above set forth for the registering of this grant, within the time herein above limited for the completion thereof; or if the said **William Bay**, his heirs, or assigns, shall not pay to us , our heirs and successors, or to the Receiver General of our quit-rents, or to the proper officer appointed to receive the same, the said quit-rent of one halfpenny sterling per acre, on the said feast of St. Michael, or with fourteen days after, annually, for every acre contained in this grant; that then, and in either of these cases, respectively, this grant shall be void, anything

herein contained to the contrary notwithstanding; and the said lands, tenements, hereditaments, and premises being specified, and every part and parcel thereof, shall revert to us, our heirs, and successors, fully and absolutely, as if the same had never been granted.

(ASP 8:1:601)

Abstract A: NON-RESIDENT BRITISH GRANTS

Register's Number: 31
Present Claimants: **Elihu Hall Bay**
Original Grantees/Claimants: **Elihu Hal l Bay**
Acreage/Location: 1,100 ; on the river Homochitto
Patent Date: 27 September 1773

Register's Number: 32
Present Claimants: **Elihu Hall Bay**
Original Grantees/Claimants: **William Garnier**
Acreage/Location: 4,800; on the waters of river Homochitto
Patent Date: 28 May 1779

Register's Number: 33
Present Claimants: **Elihu Hall Bay**
Original Grantees/Claimants: **William Grant**
Acreage/Location: 1,000; River Mississippi
Patent Date: 6 May 1776

Register's Number: 34
Present Claimants: **Elihu Hall Bay**
Original Grantees/Claimants: **William Grant**
Acreage/Location: 1,000 ; Walnut hills
Patent Date: 6 May 1776

Register's Number: 35
Present Claimants: **Elihu Hall Bay**
Original Grantees/Claimants: **Doctor John Lorimer**
Acreage/Location: 2,000; Walnut hills
Patent Date: 6 May 1776

Register's Number: 40
Present Claimants: **Elihu Hall Bay**
Original Grantees/Claimants: **John Smith**
Acreage/Location: 600; on Cole's creek
Patent Date: 22 July 1769

Register's Number: 216
Present Claimants: **Elihu Hall Bay**
Original Grantees/Claimants: **James Barbour**
Acreage/Location: 250; on Second creek
Patent Date: 13 September 1775

Register's Number: 38
Present Claimants: **Elihu Hall Bay**
Original Grantees/Claimants: **Amos Ogden**
Acreage/Location: 1,575; on the river Homochitto
Patent Date: 27 October 1772

Register's Number: 39
Present Claimants: **Elihu Hall Bay**
Original Grantees/Claimants: **Amos Ogden**
Acreage/Location: 1,500; on Buffalo creek
Patent Date: 6 May 1774

Register's Number: 36
Present Claimants: **Elihu Hall Bay**
Original Grantees/Claimants: **Thaddeus Lyman**
Acreage/Location: 1,050; on the Bayou Pierre
Patent Date: 2 February 1775

Register's Number: 37
Present Claimants: **Elihu Hall Bay**
Original Grantees/Claimants: **Thaddeus Lyman**
Acreage/Location: 1, 050; on the Bayou Pierre
Patent Date: 2 February 1775

Register's Number: 1,493
Present Claimants: **Elihu Hall Bay**
Original Grantees/Claimants: **James Marcus Prevost**
Acreage/Location: 750; on the river Mississippi
Patent Date: 14 July 1778

Register's Number: 1,494
Present Claimants: **Elihu Hall Bay** and **Robert J. Turnbull**
Original Grantees/Claimants: **William Bay**
Acreage/Location: 1,100; on the river Mississippi
Patent Date: 22 November 1776

Register's Number: 19
Present Claimants: **Alexander Macullagh**
Original Grantees/Claimants: **William Fricker**
Acreage/Location: 500; on Buffalo creek
Patent Date: 8 November 1777

Register's Number: 20
Present Claimants: **Alexander Macullagh**
Original Grantees/Claimants: **John Southwell**
Acreage/Location: 1,000; on the waters of Buffalo creek
Patent Date: 2 August 1773

Register's Number: 21
Present Claimants: **Alexander Macullagh**
Original Grantees/Claimants: **Patrick Kelly**
Acreage/Location: 200; on Boyd's or Cole's creek
Patent Date: 2 September 1779

Register's Number: 217
Present Claimants: **Alexander Macullagh**
Original Grantees/Claimants: **William Grant**
Acreage/Location: 1,000; on the river Mississippi
Patent Date: 2 October 1778

Register's Number: 1,566
Present Claimants: **Alexander Macullagh**
Original Grantees/Claimants: **James M. Prevost**
Acreage/Location: 750; on the river Mississippi
Patent Date: --

Register's Number: 120
Present Claimants: **William McCaleb** and **Francis Bremarr**
Original Grantees/Claimants: **William Marshall**
Acreage/Location: 600; on the waters of Fairchild's creek
Patent Date: 24 March 1777

Register's Number: 119
Present Claimants: **John Southwell,** legal representatives of
Original Grantees/Claimants: **John Southwell**
Acreage/Location: 900; on Buffalo creek
Patent Date: 2 Aug 1773

Register's Number: 1,489
Present Claimants: **John Stephenson**
Original Grantees/Claimants: **John Stephenson**
Acreage/Location: 1,200; on Boyd's or Cole's creek
Patent Date: 28 February 1778

Register's Number: 1,490
Present Claimants: **John Scott,** legal representatives of
Original Grantees/Claimants: **John Scott**
Acreage/Location: 1,000; on the river Mississippi
Patent Date: 24 July 1772

Register's Number: 591
Present Claimants: **Thomas James**
Original Grantees/Claimants: **Thomas James**
Acreage/Location: 200; on the river Mississippi
Patent Date: 6 May 1776

Register's Number: 592
Present Claimants: **Thomas James**
Original Grantees/Claimants: **Susanna Jacobs**
Acreage/Location: 200; on the river Mississippi
Patent Date: 8 September 1775

Register's Number: 593
Present Claimants: **Thomas James**
Original Grantees/Claimants: **Thomas James**
Acreage/Location: 500; on the Bayou Pierre
Patent Date: 15 Aug 1777

Register's Number: 598
Present Claimants: **James Hughes**
Original Grantees/Claimants: **James Hughes**
Acreage/Location: 1,000; on St. Catherine's creek
Patent Date: 26 April 1779

Register's Number: 599
Present Claimants: **James Hughes**
Original Grantees/Claimants: **James Hughes**
Acreage/Location: 550; on Boyd's or Cole's creek
Patent Date: 6 January 1778

Register's Number: 688
Present Claimants: **Oliver Pollock**
Original Grantees/Claimants: **Jeremiah Germain**
Acreage/Location: 200; on Second creek
Patent Date: 20 November 1776

Register's Number: 761
Present Claimants: **Augustine Prevost**
Original Grantees/Claimants: **Augustine Prevost**
Acreage/Location: 1,000; on Cole's creek
Patent Date: 30 March 1778

Register's Number: 762
Present Claimants: **Augustine Prevost**
Original Grantees/Claimants: **Augustine Prevost**
Acreage/Location: 1,000; on Sandy creek
Patent Date: 16 January 1777

Register's Number: 763
Present Claimants: **Augustine Prevost**
Original Grantees/Claimants: **Augustine Prevost**
Acreage/Location: 5,000; on Cole's creek
Patent Date: 31 December 1776

Register's Number: 764
Present Claimants: **Augustine Prevost**
Original Grantees/Claimants: **Augustine Prevost**
Acreage/Location: 1,000; on the Bayou Fonica
Patent Date: 15 September 1777

Register's Number: 765
Present Claimants: **Augustine Prevost**
Original Grantees/Claimants: **Augustine Prevost**
Acreage/Location: 1,000; on Cole's creek
Patent Date: 30 March 1778

Register's Number: 1,078
Present Claimants: **William Collins**
Original Grantees/Claimants: **William Collins**
Acreage/Location: 200; on the waters of Cole's creek
Patent Date: 20 March 1778

Register's Number: 1,136
Present Claimants: **Robert Farmer,** deceased, legal representatives of
Original Grantees/Claimants: **Robert Farmer**
Acreage/Location: 3,000; on Sandy creek
Patent Date: 22 September 1775

Register's Number: 1,755
Present Claimants: **Robert Callender,** deceased, legal representatives of
Original Grantees/Claimants: **Robert Callender**
Acreage/Location: 2000; at Lofftus cliffs
Patent Date: 6 December 1768

Register's Number: 1,892
Present Claimants: **Thomas Durham,** deceased, legal representatives of
Original Grantees/Claimants: **John Blommart**
Acreage/Location: 2,000; on the waters of Fairchild's creek
Patent Date: 29 April 1777

Register's Number: 1,896
Present Claimants: **Richard Barry**
Original Grantees/Claimants: **Richard Barry**
Acreage/Location: 50; on Cole's creek
Patent Date: 22 July 1769

Register's Number: 1,897
Present Claimants: **William Mills**
Original Grantees/Claimants: **William Mills**
Acreage/Location: 50; on Cole's creek
Patent Date: 22 July 1769

Register's Number: 1, 898
Present Claimants: **David Hodge,** deceased, legal representatives of
Original Grantees/Claimants: **James Ramsey**
Acreage/Location: 1,000; on Cole's creek
Patent Date: 26 March 1774

Register's Number: 1,899
Present Claimants: **James Amoss***
Original Grantees/Claimants: **James Amos*** [*so spelled]
Acreage/Location: 600; Lofftus cliffs
Patent Date: 24 July 1772

Register's Number: 1,900
Present Claimants: **Sylvester** and **James Fanning**, legal representatives of
Original Grantees/Claimants: **Sylvester** and **James Fanning**
Acreage/Location: 2,000; near Lofftus cliffs
Patent Date: 15 December 1768

Register's Number: 1,901
Present Claimants: **David Hodge,** deceased, legal representatives of
Original Grantees/Claimants: **John Sommers**
Acreage/Location: 2,000; Buffalo creek
Patent Date: 20 January 1778

(ASP 8:1:602)

Register's Number: 1,902
Present Claimants: **David Hodge,** deceased, legal representatives of
Original Grantees/Claimants: **Andrew Ransford**
Acreage/Location: 1,250; on the river Mississippi
Patent Date: 12 May 1773

Register's Number: 1,903
Present Claimants: **Richard Freeman Pearne**
Original Grantees/Claimants: **Richard Freeman Pearne**
Acreage/Location: 50; on Cole's creek
Patent Date: 22 July 1769

Register's Number: 1,904
Present Claimants: **David Hodge,** deceased, legal representatives of
Original Grantees/Claimants: **Frederick Haldermand**
Acreage/Location: 2,000; on the river Mobile
Patent Date: 17 January 1770

Register's Number: 1,906
Present Claimants: **Edward Todd**
Original Grantees/Claimants: **Alexander McIntosh**
Acreage/Location: 500; Petit Gulph creek
Patent Date: 6 March 1670* [*sic; 1770 must have been meant]

Register's Number: 1,953
Present Claimants: **Daniel Ward,** deceased, legal representatives of
Original Grantees/Claimants: **Daniel Ward**
Acreage/Location: 1,500; on the river Mississippi
Patent Date: 24 November 1768

Register's Number: 1,954
Present Claimants: **Daniel Ward,** deceased, legal representatives of
Original Grantees/Claimants: **William Fricker**
Acreage/Location: 500; on the waters of Cole's Creek
Patent Date: 8 November 1777

Register's Number: 1,967
Present Claimants: **Joshua Ward**
Original Grantees/Claimants: **Joshua Ward**
Acreage/Location: 600; on the river Mississippi
Patent Date: 21 November 1768

Register's Number: 775
Present Claimants: **Joseph W. A. Lloyd**
Original Grantees/Claimants: **James Barbour**
Acreage/Location: 250; on Second creek
Patent Date: 13 September 1775

Register's Number: 909
Present Claimants: **Philip Alston**
Original Grantees/Claimants: **Thomas Fry**
Acreage/Location: 200; on Petit Gulph creek
Patent Date: 7 July 1775

Register's Number: 975
Present Claimants: **Ann Carr**
Original Grantees/Claimants: **John Firby**
Acreage/Location: 1,000; on Cole's creek
Patent Date: 23 September 1779

Register's Number: 974
Present Claimants: **William Godley**
Original Grantees/Claimants: **William Godley**
Acreage/Location: 250; on the river Mississippi
Patent Date: 21 October 1774

Register's Number: 1,139
Present Claimants: -- **Rhea** and -- **Cochran**
Original Grantees/Claimants: **Thomas Hutchins**
Acreage/Location: 400; on the river Homochitto
Patent Date: 24 October 1774

Register's Number: 1,231
Present Claimants: **Elijah Cushing**
Original Grantees/Claimants: **Ephraim Thornell**
Acreage/Location: 100; on Second creek
Patent Date: 12 November 1778

Register's Number: 1,364
Present Claimants: **John Ogden**
Original Grantees/Claimants: **Amos Ogden**
Acreage/Location: 3,000; on the river Homochitto
Patent Date: 6 May 1774

Register's Number: 1,491
Present Claimants: **David Waugh's** heirs
Original Grantees/Claimants: **David Waugh**
Acreage/Location: 1000; on St. Catherine's Creek
Patent Date: 11 March 1777

Register's Number: 1,492
Present Claimants: **Thomas Hardy,** deceased, legal representatives of
Original Grantees/Claimants: **Thomas Hardy**
Acreage/Location: 500; on the river Mississippi
Patent Date: 4 July 1769

Register's Number: 1,877
Present Claimants: **Solomon Alston**
Original Grantees/Claimants: **John Alston**
Acreage/Location: 450; near Natchez
Patent Date: 16 June 1777

Register's Number: 1,879
Present Claimants: **Absalom Hooper**
Original Grantees/Claimants: **Absalom Hooper**
Acreage/Location: 250; on Second creek
Patent Date: 21 September 1772

Register's Number: 1,916
Present Claimants: **Jacob Winfree**
Original Grantees/Claimants: **Jacob Winfree**
Acreage/Location: 1,000; on Second creek
Patent Date: 7 July 1773

Register's Number: 1,937
Present Claimants: **Sir George Brydges Rodney**, deceased, legal representatives of
Original Grantees/Claimants: **Sir George Brydges Rodney**
Acreage/Location: 5,000; on the river Mississippi
Patent Date: 27 May ----

Register's Number: 986
Present Claimants: **James Ferguson,** for the use of **Benjamin Farrar**
Original Grantees/Claimants: **James Ferguson**
Acreage/Location: 600; on Second creek
Patent Date: 21 September 1772

Register's Number: 992
Present Claimants: **Edward Evan** and **James Jones**
Original Grantees/Claimants: **Thaddeus Lyman**
Acreage/Location: 666+; on the Bayou Pierre
Patent Date: 2 February 1775

Register's Number: 1,024
Present Claimants: **Daniel Hughes,** agent for **William Johnson**
Original Grantees/Claimants: **James Barbour**
Acreage/Location: 500; on Second creek
Patent Date: 13 September 1773

Register's Number: 1,244
Present Claimants: **Joseph King,** deceased, legal representatives of
Original Grantees/Claimants: **Amos Ogden**
Acreage/Location: 1,000; on the river Homochitto
Patent Date: 27 October 1772

Register's Number: 1, 363
Present Claimants: **Amos Ogden,** legal representatives of
Original Grantees/Claimants: **Amos Ogden**
Acreage/Location: 4,500; on the river Homochitto
Patent Date: 27 October 1772

Register's Number: 1,649
Present Claimants: **Tench Cox**
Original Grantees/Claimants: **Thaddeus Lyman**
Acreage/Location: 333+; on the Bayou Pierre
Patent Date: 2 February 1775

Register's Number: 976
Present Claimants: **Thomas Wadsworth,** deceased, legal representatives of
Original Grantees/Claimants: **William Marshall**
Acreage/Location: 2,000; ----
Patent Date: 5 June 1778

Register's Number: 977
Present Claimants: **Samuel Holliday**
Original Grantees/Claimants: **Amos Ogdon**
Acreage/Location: 1,000; on the river Homochitto
Patent Date: 27 October 1772

Register's Number: 1,844
Present Claimants: **John Armstreet**
Original Grantees/Claimants: **William Garnier**
Acreage/Location: 200; on the waters of the river Homochitto
Patent Date: 28 May 1779

Register's Number: 2,027
Present Claimants: **Thomas Hutchins, Junior**
Original Grantees/Claimants: **Thomas Hutchins, Senior**
Acreage/Location: 200; on the river Homochitto
Patent Date: 21 October 1774

Register's Number: 2,034
Present Claimants: **Lorenzo Dow**
Original Grantees/Claimants: **Joseph Jackson**
Acreage/Location: 500; Briar creek
Patent Date: 21 July 1778

Register's Number: 2,033
Present Claimants: **Lorenzo Dow**
Original Grantees/Claimants: **Joseph Jackson**
Acreage/Location: 100; Briar creek
Patent Date: 21 July 1778

(ASP 8:1: 603)

The Commissioners appointed east of Pearl river , "for ascertaining the rights of persons claiming the benefit of the articles of agreement and cession between the United States and the State of Georgia, or of the first three sections" of an act entitled "An act regulating the grants of land, and providing for the disposal of the lands of the United States south of the State of Tennessee,"

British grants legally and fully executed, and duly recorded, in conformity to the provisions of said act, and not confirmed to the holders thereof under the articles of agreement and cessions above mentioned.

Original Grantee: **John McIntosh**
Present Claimant: **John McIntosh, heirs of**
Date of Grant: 12 September 1775
Acreage: 500
Present Situation of the Land: It is covered by a certificate issued by the Board to **Ann Lawrence**, legal representative of **Moses Moore**, in virtue of a Spanish warrant or order of survey
Conditions Annexed to Grant: [There follows a lengthy recital similar to those in "Conditions", Paragraph One, above]
Evidence of Grant Fulfilment: It appears, from the endorsement on the grant, that it was duly registered in the Register's Office. **John McGrew, Esq.,** testified that **John McIntosh** had land cleared, and negroes working on said land in the year 1780, or 1781, and that it was said that the land was cultivated at that time for account of **John McIntosh**. **Thomas Bassett** deposed "that he knew that said land was inhabited and cultivated at the time the British held this country, by his, **McIntosh**'s, negroes and overseers."
Remarks: [None]

(ASP 8:1:604)

Original Grantee: **Abraham Little**
Present Claimant: **Francis Coleman**
Date of Grant: 16 February 1778
Acreage: 100
Present Situation of the Land: It is covered in part by a donation certificate issued by the Board in favor of **John McGrew, Senior**
Conditions Annexed to Grant: Same as the preceding
Evidence of Grant Fulfilment: It appears from the endorsement on the grant, that it was duly registered in the Register's Office and docketed in the Auditor's Office. No evidence of the fulfilment of the other conditions of the grant.
Remarks: [None]

(ASP 8:1:605)

Original Grantee: **Robert Farmer**
Present Claimant: **Robert Farmer, heirs of**
Date of Grant: 6 August 1778
Acreage: 1,000
Present Situation of the Land: It is covered by the following certificates of pre-emption issued by the Board; one in the name of **Rawleigh Green**; one in the name of **Peter Cartwright**, one in the name of **John Pickering**; ine in the name of **Jos[eph] Westmoreland**; and a donation certificate in the name of **Clark McGrew**

Conditions Annexed to Grant: conditions same as preceding
Evidence of Grant Fulfilment: same as next preceding
Remarks: --

Original Grantee: **Robert Farmer**
Present Claimant: **Robert Farmer, heirs of**
Date of Grant: 6 August [1778]
Acreage: 800
Present Situation of the Land: It is covered in part by a pre-emption certificate issued by the Board in the name of **Charles Cassiter**
Conditions Annexed to Grant: Conditions same as the preceding
Evidence of Grant Fulfilment: Same as the next preceding
Remarks: --

Original Grantee: **Peter De Forge**
Present Claimant: **Peter De Forge, heirs of**
Date of Grant: 16 April 1779
Acreage: 100
Present Situation of the Land: Not known
Conditions Annexed to Grant: Conditions same as the preceding
Evidence of Grant Fulfilment: Same as the next preceding
Remarks: --

Original Grantee: **Allen Grant**
Present Claimant: **Theodore Gilliard**
Date of Grant: 4 October [1779]
Acreage: 100
Present Situation of the Land: Not known
Conditions Annexed to Grant: Conditions same as the preceding
Evidence of Grant Fulfilment: Same as the next preceding
Remarks: --

Original Grantee: **John Sutherland**
Present Claimant: **Elihu Hall Bay**
Date of Grant: 22 October [1779]
Acreage: 500
Present Situation of the Land: It is covered in part by the following certificates issued by the Board: a pre-emption certificate in the name of **Peter Malone**; a pre-emption certificate in the name of **Edward Lt. Wailes**; and a certificate in virtue of a Spanish warrant, or order of survey, in the name of **John Baker**
Conditions Annexed to Grant: Conditions same as the preceding, except that the payment of the quit-rent commences within ten years after the feast of St. Michael which may first happen after the date of the grant, instead of two years, as in the preceding cases
Evidence of Grant Fulfilment: Same as in the next preceding
Remarks: --

Original Grantee: **William Fradgely**
Present Claimant: **Elihu Hall Bay**
Date of Grant: 13 March 1776
Acreage: 27
Present Situation of the Land: It is covered by a certificate issued by the Board in favor of **John Johnston,** in virtue of a Spanish warrant, or order of survey
Conditions Annexed to Grant: Conditions same as the preceding
Evidence of Grant Fulfilment: Same as the next preceding
Remarks: --

(ASP 8:1:606)

Original Grantee: **William Fradgely**
Present Claimant: **Elihu Hall Bay**
Date of Grant: 13 March 1776
Acreage: 173
Present Situation of the Land: It is covered by a certificate issued by the Board in favor of **Ann Lawrence**, representative of **Moses Moore**, in virtue of a Spanish warrant, or order of survey, and a certificate in virtue of a Spanish warrant in the name of **Cornelius Rain**
Conditions Annexed to Grant: Conditions the same as the preceding
Evidence of Grant Fulfilment: Same as the next preceding
Remarks: --

Original Grantee: **George Burdon**
Present Claimant: **George Burdon**
Date of Grant: 17 August 1779
Acreage: 200
Present Situation of the Land: Not known
Conditions Annexed to Grant: Conditions same as preceding
Evidence of Grant Fulfilment: Same as the next preceding
Remarks: --

Original Grantee: **George Burdon**
Present Claimant: **George Burdon**
Date of Grant: 17 August 1779
Acreage: 800
Present Situation of the Land: Not known
Conditions Annexed to Grant: Conditions same as the preceding
Evidence of Grant Fulfilment: Same as the next preceding
Remarks: --

Original Grantee: **Alex[ander] Macullagh**
Present Claimant: **Alex[ander] Macullagh,** nephew and heir
Date of Grant: 6 April 1778
Acreage: 200
Present Situation of the Land: It is covered by a certificate issued by the Board in favor of **Daniel Johnson**, under a Spanish warrant, or order of survey
Conditions Annexed to Grant: Conditions same as the preceding
Evidence of Grant Fulfilment: Same as the next preceding
Remarks: --

Original Grantee: **William Clark**
Present Claimant: **Samuel Mims**
Date of Grant: 6 August [1778]
Acreage: 350
Present Situation of the Land: It is inhabited and cultivated by **Samuel Mims**. No other claim exhibited therefore
Conditions Annexed to Grant: [Recites "Conditions", Paragraph 1]
Evidence of Grant Fulfilment: Same as the next preceding
Remarks: It has been stated in proof to us, that **Samuel Mims**, the present claimant, has been in the continued and peaceable possession, cultivation, and habitation of this land for the last eighteen or twenty years, either as the tenant of **William Clark**, the original grantee, or as a purchaser under said -- **Clark**; but we were of opinion, that the chain of title from -- **Clark** to -- **Mims,** is incomplete. See journal, Present Claimant:, page 436. We had no evidence that **William Clark** was resident within the ceded territory on the 27th day of October 1795. There has been no other claim for this land, or any part of it, presented to us.

Original Grantee: **John Lott, Junior**
Present Claimant: **William Vardiman**
Date of Grant: 16 February 1778
Acreage: 300
Present Situation of the Land: It is covered by a certificate issued by the Board, in the name of **James Caller**, in virtue of a Spanish warrant, and a donation certificate in the name of **Noah Kenner Hutson**, in the occupancy of **William Vardiman,** the holder of the British grant.
Conditions Annexed to Grant: Conditions same as the next preceding.
Evidence of Grant Fulfilment: Same as the next preceding.
Remarks: Same as the next preceding.

Original Grantee: **William Wall**
Present Claimant: **James Hoggatt**
Date of Grant: 20 March 1778
Acreage: 250
Present Situation of the Land: It is covered by a certificate issued by the Board in the name of **James Caller** in virtue of a Spanish warrant.
Conditions Annexed to Grant: Conditions same as the next preceding.

Evidence of Grant Fulfilment: It appears from the endorsements on this grant, that it was duly registered in the Register's Office, and docketed in the Auditor's Office. **John McGrew, Esq.**, deposed "that **James Hoggatt**, lived on the land and that said **Hoggatt** had a plantation and barn on said place." **Thomas Bassett** testified " that he knew that **James Hoggatt** lived on the land in the year 1789 or before that time."

Remarks: --

(ASP 8:1:608)

Original Grantee: **Charles Walker**
Present Claimant: **Francis Coleman**
Date of Grant: 27 January 1777
Acreage: 500
Present Situation of the Land: It is covered by a certificate issued by the Board in the name of **John Baker**, in virtue of a Spanish warrant, and a donation certificate in the name of **John McGrew, Senior.**
Conditions Annexed to Grant: Conditions same as the next preceding
Evidence of Grant Fulfilment: It appears from the endorsement on this grant that it was duly registered in the Register's Office. **John McGrew, Senior,** deposed "that he knew that **Charles Walker** settled upon this land in our about the year 1778, built a house, and made two or three crops thereon; and he believed had cleared and under cultivation within the limits of the grants, about forty acres.
Remarks: --

[The schedule for the above-listed grants was prepared by the Board of Commissioners, East of Pearl River, 14 September 1805, and signed by **Ro[bert] C. Nicholas** and **Joseph Chambers**, Commissioners and sent to the Hon. **Albert Gallatin, Esq.**, Secretary of the Treasury]

(ASP:1:609)

Abstract of British Claims entered with the Register of the Land Office west of Pearl River, under the fifth section of an act entitled "An act further to amend an act entitled An act regulating the grants of land, and providing for the disposal of the lands of the United States south of the State of Tennessee

Register's Number: 2083
Present Claimant: **Thomas Davy**
Original Grantee/Claimant: **Weston Varlo**
Acreage: 1,000
Situation: On the waters of the Bayou Pierre
Patent Date: The original patent to **Weston Varlo** for these three tracts have never been filed in this office; deeds of lease and release being the only evidence of title exhibited.

Register's Number: 2084
Present Claimant: **Thomas Davy**
Original Grantee/Claimant: **Weston Varlo**
Acreage: 1,000
Situation: As per preceding grant
Patent Date: As per preceding grant

Register's Number: 2085
Present Claimant: **Thomas Davy**
Original Grantee/Claimant: **Weston Varlo**
Acreage: 500
Situation: As per preceding grant
Patent Date: As per preceding grant

Register's Number: 2086
Present Claimant: **Thomas Davy**
Original Grantee/Claimant: **David Dickson**
Acreage: 1,000
Situation: On the river Homochitto
Patent Date: 27 September 1773

Register's Number: 2087
Present Claimant: **William Wilton**
Original Grantee/Claimant: **William Wilton**
Acreage: 500
Situation: On the river Homochitto
Patent Date: 17 October 1774

Register's Number: 2088
Present Claimant: **William Wilton**
Original Grantee/Claimant: **William Marshall**
Acreage: 400
Situation: On Fairchild's creek
Patent Date: 24 March 1777. Part of a grant of 1000 acres. The residue of the tract is claimed by **William McCaleb** and **F. Bremarr,** by whom the original patent was filed, under the act of 1803, and reported by the Commissioners, and numbered 120.

Register's Number: 2089
Present Claimant: **William Wilton**
Original Grantee/Claimant: **James Barbut**
Acreage: 200
Situation: On Second creek
Patent Date: 13 September 1775. The original patent for 1000 acres, filed by **E[lihu] H[all] Bay** and by **J. A.W. Lloyd**. See Commissioner's Numbers 216 and 773. This land is also

claimed by **William Johnson**; see Number 1024. Deeds of conveyance, however, for the quantity here claimed, have been filed by the present claimant.

Register's Number: 2090
Present Claimant: **William Wilton**
Original Grantee/Claimant: **William Fricker**
Acreage: 500
Situation: On Cole's creek
Patent Date: 8 November 1777. The original patent for 2000 acres, filed by **A. Macullagh** and **Daniel Ward's heirs;** See Numbers 15 and 1954, who claim a moiety of the entire tract; there appears to be 500 acres for which no claim has been set up.

Register's Number: 2091
Present Claimant: **William Clark,** legal representatives of
Original Grantee/Claimant: **Daniel Ryan**
Acreage: 100
Situation: On Briar creek [District East of Pearl river]
Patent Date: 23 April 1777. No conveyance from the patentee produced.

Register's Number: 2092
Present Claimant: **William Clark,** legal representatives of
Original Grantee/Claimant: **William Clark**
Acreage: 576
Situation: On the river Alabama [District East of Pearl river]
Patent Date: 22 October 1779

Register's Number: 2093
Present Claimant: **William Clark,** legal representatives of
Original Grantee/Claimant: **James Peterkin**
Acreage: 500
Situation: On the river Pascagola {District East of Pearl river]
Patent Date: 29 December 1778. No conveyance from the patentee produced.

Register's Number: 2094
Present Claimant: **Anthony Francis Halderman**
Original Grantee/Claimant: **Frederick Halderman**
Acreage: 500
Situation: Near the Natchez
Patent Date: There are no papers filed in this and following two claims. **Halderman's** attorney has presented unauthenticated plots of the land, stated to be copied from the original plots of the Surveyor General.

Register's Number: 2095
Present Claimant: **Anthony Francis Halderman**
Original Grantee/Claimant: **Frederick Halderman**
Acreage: 500
Situation: Near the Natchez
Patent Date: See Register's Number 2094

Register's Number: 2096
Present Claimant: **Anthony Francis Halderman**
Original Grantee/Claimant: **Frederick Halderman**
Acreage: 500
Situation: On the river Mississippi
Patent Date: See Register's Number 2094

Register's Number: 2097
Present Claimant: **John Peck**
Original Grantee/Claimant: **Thaddeus Lyman**
Acreage: 6500
Situation: On the Bayou Pierre
Patent Date: Present Claimant: February 1775. Part of **Lyman's** mandamus, which was confiscated by the Spanish Government, and has been confirmed to the present settlers in possession, by the Board of Commissioners

Register's Number: 2098
Present Claimant: **The Earl of Eglinton,** legal representatives of
Original Grantee/Claimant: **Earl of Eglinton**
Acreage: 20,000
Situation: Near the Natchez
Patent Date: A transcript from the British records, stating that a grant had issued to the Earl of Eglinton for this land, is the only evidence of title exhibited. This was presented by **John McCaleb,** on behalf of the heirs, but no power of attorney, or other document, proving him to be invested with authority to act was ever shown. The land is entirely covered by Spanish patents, being one of the most flourishing settlements in this district.

The foregoing is a list of all the claims filed in this office, under the fifth section of the act of 2nd March 1805. Land Ofice West of Pearl River, 26 July 1808. [Signed:] **Thomas H. Williams,** Register of the Land Office.

(8:1:610)

B.

Abstract of Spanish Grants disallowed, on suspicion of being antedated.

Register's Number: 507
Present Claimants: **William Vousdan,** deceased, legal representatives of
Original Grantees or Claimants: **William Vousdan**
Quantity in arpents: 2,000
Situation: On the Bayou Sara
Patent Date: 30 August 1793

Register's Number: 1400
Present Claimants: **Robert Moore**
Original Grantees or Claimants: **Robert Moore**
Quantity in arpents: 1,000
Situation: On the Bayou Sara
Patent Date: 26 December 1795

Register's Number: 1425
Present Claimants: **James Moore,** in right of his wife **Maria [Moore]**
Original Grantees or Claimants: **Maria Whittle**
Quantity in arpents: 700
Situation: On the Bayou Sara
Patent Date: 18 June 1795

Register's Number: 1753
Present Claimants: **Thomas Burling**
Original Grantees or Claimants: **Thomas Burling**
Quantity in arpents: 1,000
Situation: On the Bayou Sara
Patent Date: 18 June 1795

Register's Number: 1420
Present Claimants: **James Moore**
Original Grantees or Claimants: **James Moore**
Quantity in arpents: 1,000
Situation: On the Bayou Sara
Patent Date: 26 December 1795

Register's Number: 1368
Present Claimants: **Samuel P. Moore, James Moore,** and **Robert Moore**
Original Grantees or Claimants: **Sarah Scott**
Quantity in arpents: 1,000
Situation: On the Bayou Sara
Patent Date: 22 March 1795

Register's Number: 1370
Present Claimants: **Samuel P. Moore, James Moore,** and **Robert Moore**
Original Grantees or Claimants: **William Moore**
Quantity in arpents: 1,000
Situation: On the Bayou Sara
Patent Date: 22 March 1795

Register's Number: 1379
Present Claimants: **William Scott**
Original Grantees or Claimants: **William Scott**
Quantity in arpents: 1,000
Situation: On the Bayou Sara
Patent Date: 20 March 1795

Register's Number: 1097
Present Claimants: **Abijah Hunt**
Original Grantees or Claimants: **James White**
Quantity in arpents: 1,300
Situation: On Well's creek
Patent Date: 20 January 1795

Register's Number: 394
Present Claimants: **Nicholas G. Ridgley**
Original Grantees or Claimants: **James White**
Quantity in arpents: 625
Situation: On Well's creek
Patent Date: 20 January 1795

Register's Number: 1657
Present Claimants: **Edward Evans**
Original Grantees or Claimants: **James White**
Quantity in arpents: 280
Situation: On Well's creek
Patent Date: 20 January 1795

Register's Number: 1637
Present Claimants: **Henry Garvey**
Original Grantees or Claimants: **Henry Garvey**
Quantity in arpents: 200
Situation: On Well's creek
Patent Date: 25 January 1795

Register's Number: 1638
Present Claimants: **Henry Garvey**
Original Grantees or Claimants: **Henry Garvey**
Quantity in arpents: 330
Situation: River Homochitto
Patent Date: 25 January 1795

Register's Number: 1111
Present Claimants: **Abijah Hunt**
Original Grantees or Claimants: **William Lewis**
Quantity in arpents: 500
Situation: On the Bayou Sara
Patent Date: 20 March 1795

Register's Number: 1141
Present Claimants: **Margaret Thompson**
Original Grantees or Claimants: **Margaret Thompson**
Quantity in arpents: 1,000
Situation: On the Bayou Pierre
Patent Date: 2 December 1797

Register's Number: 1142
Present Claimants: **Jacintha Vidal,** deceased, legal representatives of
Original Grantees or Claimants: **Jacintha Gallagher**
Quantity in arpents: 1,000
Situation: On the Bayou Pierre
Patent Date: 2 December 1797

Register's Number: 1140
Present Claimants: **Thomas Thompson**
Original Grantees or Claimants: **Thomas Thompson**
Quantity in arpents: 800
Situation: On the Bayou Pierre
Patent Date: 2 December 1797

Register's Number: 1403
Present Claimants: **Nicholas Kemplin**
Original Grantees or Claimants: **Nicholas Kemplin**
Quantity in arpents: 400
Situation: On the Bayou Sara
Patent Date: 22 March 1795

Register's Number: 1728
Present Claimants: **William Dunbar**
Original Grantees or Claimants: **William Dunbar**
Quantity in arpents: Lot No. 3
Situation: On square No. 26 in the city of Natchez
Patent Date: Situation: December 1794

(ASP 8:1:611)

D.

Report of Claims founded on British and Spanish Warrants of Survey within the District west of Pearl River, disallowed by the Board of Commissioners; made in pursuance of the fourth section of an act, entitled "An act concerning the sales of the lands of the United States, and for other purposes," passed 31 March 1808.

Register's No.: 4
Present Claimant: **William Conway**
Original Claimant: **Maurice Conway**
Situation: Buffalo Creek
Quantity: 800*f*
Title, Whence Derived: Spanish
Title Dated: 1 October 1788
Remarks: No evidence offered.

Register's No.: 25
Present Claimant: **Thomas Green**
Original Claimant: **Thomas Green**
Situation: Near Natchez
Quantity: 100*f*
Title, Whence Derived: This land was regranted by the Spanish Government, and a patent issued to **Peter Piernas, Esq.**, 24 February 1783. The claim was confirmed by the Board to **Robert Cochran**, assignee of the patentee.
— **Thomas M. Green** says, "that he was present, and saw the Spanish surveyor run the two first lines the lengthy and breadth of said land, beginning at a stake, a made corner. The surveyor

marked the name of the claimant in initials on one of the corner trees, and delivered possession of the land to the claimant; and then the deponent left the ground. The said deponent says, that the said Thomas Green was twenty-one years of age, and the head of a family, on 1st September 1782."

-- **William Barland** says, "that he was present, towit, in the fall of 1782, when the survey of said land was about to be run. He saw the stake and a made corner stuck in the ground, and saw the surveyor start; and then he went away. The next day he attended, and saw the survey finished. The said deponent further says, that he understood, by common report, that the Spanish commandant had rented, or had obtained leave of said Thomas Green to use said land as a pasture; and the said deponent saw the Spanish troops putting a fence round said premises for said commandant. A few days after the said survey was made, the same surveyor run out a tract of land for said witness, and made one of said Thomas Green's lines a boundary for this deponent's line."

-- **Palser Schilling** says, "that he was in the surveyor's office, where they showed him the plan or plot of the tract of land in question, included in a general map of the lands granted or surveyed in this country by the Spanish Government. This deponent further says, that he knows that the said Thomas Moore and all his slaves, property, and papers were seized upon by the Spanish commandant, and sent to New Orleans, and that it was a general practice of said commandant, and seize upon papers in particular, and to select and destroy such as he thought proper."

-- **Stephen Minor** says "that the claimant was the head of a family at the date of the warrant; that he never inhabited or cultivated this land; that, on the arrival of Peter Piernas, Lieutenant Governor under the Spanish Government at Natches, on or about the year 1784, he requested the witness to apply to the claimant to lethim have a part of the land in question, to make a pasture for his horses, who consented, and a parcel thereof was fenced in accordingly by the said Piernas, and used as such; and the witness saw the surveyor general, **Charles Trudeau**, go out with the claimant to survey the said tract of land, and believes he did survey it for the said Green."

Title Dated: 1 September 1782
Remarks: See above

Register's No.: 49
Present Claimant: **Heirs of Robert Cloyd**
Original Claimant: **Robert Cloyd**
Situation: Bayou Pierre
Quantity: 1,000*f*
Title, Whence Derived: Spanish
Title Dated: 14 March 1794*
Remarks: --

*This warrant was issued by the local governor of the district, and not by the governor-general of the province. **Catura Wallis** says, "that, soon after the grant was obtained, the grantee died, and left a wife and five small children. The witness heard his wife complain, at the time of his decease, that he had made a small improvement on the land, and that was left unable to continue it. **Harrison Person** says, "that about two years ago (October 1803) the claimant sent for the witness to get him to endeavor to save this land for her; and proposed to him, that if he could save it, he should have one-half of it, or, that if he chose to purchase, he might have the whole for five hundred dollars. The witness took time to consider of said proposition and, before he returned to her again, she had received a letter from **Thomas Evans**, who lived nigh the premises, and refused to comply with the offer she had made to the witness, and required a return of the petition or title papers, which the witness returned about ten days afterwards. In the course of the conversation between the witness and the claimant, she acknowledged that no improvement had been made on the premises." **Cyrus Hamilton,** says, "that Robert Cloyd landed in Mississippi territory in the year 1796, some time about the month of July; and the witness does not know that he was ever in the country before, as the witness in the territory before and after that period, and never knew him, or heard of him, before that time."

(ASP 8:1:612)

Register's No.: 110
Present Claimant: **J. Bernard, heirs of**
Original Claimant: **Joseph Bernard**
Situation: Buffalo creek
Quantity: 210*f*
Title, Whence Derived: Spanish
Title Dated: 28 March 1794
Remarks: **Bennet Truly** says, "that Joseph Bernard was the head of a family at the date of the warrant."

Register's No.: 121
Present Claimant: **Benjamin Dorsey**
Original Claimant: **Benjamin Dorsey**
Situation: Homochitto river
Quantity: 500*f*
Title, Whence Derived: Spanish
Title Dated: --
Remarks: No warrant produced. This land was sold by Dorsey to **Winifred Ryan** on the 2d January 1797, and confirmed to her as a donation by the commissioners.

Register's No.: 161
Present Claimant: **Everard Green**
Original Claimant: **Everard Green**
Situation: Cole's creek
Quantity: 650*f*
Title, Whence Derived: Spanish

Title Dated: 10 February 1792

Remarks: **Thomas M. Green** says, "that the claimant was twenty-one years of age, not at the date of the warrant, but the fore part of the year 1797; that the tract of land in question is swamp land, and joins a tract of the claimant which is cultivated, but which has no timber, or not enough to support it; and that the present land was procured for the purpose of supplying timber to the tract cultivated and has been used as such ever since."

Register's No.: 259
Present Claimant: **Thomas Foster**
Original Claimant: **Thomas Foster**, patent 29 August 1817
Situation: Buffalo Creek
Quantity: 800*f*
Title, Whence Derived: Spanish
Title Dated: 14 March 1792
Remarks: **Reuben Gibson** says "that the claimant resided in the Mississippi territory on the 27th October 1795, and that he was the head of a family at the date of the warrant.

Register's No.: 285
Present Claimant: **Abraham Taylor**
Original Claimant: **Abraham Taylor**
Situation: Homochitto river
Quantity: 505*f*
Title, Whence Derived: Spanish
Title Dated: 28 March 1794
Remarks: **Joseph King** says, "that the claimant was the head of a family, at the date of the warrant, of a wife and seven or eight children."

Register's No.: 303
Present Claimant: **Jacob Harman**
Original Claimant: **Jacob Harman**
Situation: Will's creek
Quantity: 500*f*
Title, Whence Derived: Spanish
Title Dated: 24 January 1789
Remarks: No evidence offered.

Register's No.: 339
Present Claimant: **Job Corey**
Original Claimant: **Job Corey**
Situation: Cole's creek
Quantity: 100
Title Dated: --
Title, Whence Derived: British

Remarks: The original warrant was not produced, but "a certificate under the hand of **Luke Collins**, that he surveyed the land in question, in virtue of a warrant under the British Goverment; certificate dated at Opelousas in 1803." **Waterman Crane** says, "that he knows that Luke Collins was a deputy surveyor two or three years under the British Government of West Florida. The witness also says, that the claimant was the head of a family in the year 1774, and was an actual settler in the Mississippi territory on the 27th day of October 1795."

Register's No.: 346
Present Claimant: **Alexander Montgomery**
Original Claimant: **Solomon Whitley**
Situation: Homochitto river
Quantity: 400*f*
Title, Whence Derived: Spanish
Title Dated: Quantity: May 1790
Remarks: **Prosper King** says, "that Solomon Whitley was the head of a family at the date of the warrant, and the claimant began to inhabit and cultive the premises in the year 1798, by his hands, and afterwards by **Richard Crozier**, for him; and they cleared and cultivated about five acres, and built a dwelling-house, and did nothing more."-- See act of Congress passed on the 3d March 1823, "for the relief of the heirs and representatives of Alexander Montgomery, deceased," giving to the heirs and representatives of Montgomery the right to locate other land in lieu of that embraced in this order of survey.

Register's No.: 347
Present Claimant: **Alexander Montgomery**
Original Claimant: **Alexander Montgomery**
Situation: Buffalo creek
Quantity: 800*f*
Title, Whence Derived: Spanish
Title Dated: 9 July 1789
Remarks: **Prosper King** says, "that the claimant was twenty-one years of age at the date of the warrant, and was a resident in the Mississippi territory on the 27th October 1795. The claimant made a small improvement, and built a cabin on the premises, in the year 1797."

Register's No.: 368
Present Claimant: **David Corey**
Original Claimant: **David Corey**
Situation: Homochitto river
Quantity: 500*f*
Title, Whence Derived: Spanish
Title Dated: Title Dated: April 1794
Remarks: **John McCoy** says, "that the warrantee was under the age of twenty-one years on the 7th April 1794; that he was born and raised in this territory, and resided in it on the 27th day of October 1795, and ever since; that the land in question was never inhabited or cultivated until the year 1801, in which year the witness, and another hand with him, sent on the land with the

claimant, and cleared away half an acre of cane, and cut logs for a house; and nothing more has been done upon it that the witness knows of."

Register's No.: 407
Present Claimant: **T. and V. Fortner**
Original Claimant: **John Peters**
Situation: Big Black
Quantity: 240*f*
Title, Whence Derived: Spanish
Title Dated: Present Claimant: 26 April 1790
Remarks: No evidence adduced.

Register's No.: 442
Present Claimant: **Prosper King**
Original Claimant: **Prosper King**
Situation: Homochitto river
Quantity: 800*f*
Title, Whence Derived: Spanish
Title Dated: 2 March 1795
Remarks: **Alexander Montgomery** says, "that the claimant was twenty-one years of age at the date of the warrant, and, in the year 1797, the witness was on the premises, and saw a small improvement and a large stock of horses and cattle, but how long the improvement was made before that time he knows not."

Register's No.: 468
Present Claimant: **Daniel Barnet**
Original Claimant: **James Steuart**
Situation: Bayou Pierre
Quantity: 200*f*
Title, Whence Derived: Spanish
Title Dated: --
Remarks: No warrant produced, but a certificate of survey and a plot by **William Dunbar**, district surveyer, dated 19th November 1794. **Stephen Minor** says, "that James Steuart was one of the men that composed the company of dragoons under the command of **Richard King** and was entitled to the two hundred arpents for his services, and believes that the grants were generally issued to the company, as a number of them were lodged in the hands of the witness, some of which were stolen out of the house, among which might hae been the grant belonging or issued to Steuart." **Richard King** says, "that he commanded the company of horse above mentioned, and that James Steuart was one of the company, and was entitled to the two hundred arpents aforesaid; that he received a grant from Governor – **Gayoso** for the same, which the witness supposes is lost, with a number of others that were lodged with Stephen Minor, and that the warrants were generally issued to the company."

(ASP Remarks::1:613)

Register's No.: 534
Present Claimant: **John Stampley**
Original Claimant: **Hugh Matthews**
Situation: River Big Black
Quantity: 300*f*
Title, Whence Derived: Spanish
Title Dated: 24 February 1795
Remarks: **Adam Lanehart** says, "that Hugh Matthws was the head of a family at the date of the warrant, or order of survey, and that he has been an actual settler in the Mississippi territory ever since, and before that time."

Register's No.: 567
Present Claimant: **A[lexander]* Montgomery**
Original Claimant: **J[ohn] Montgomery**
Situation: River Homochitto
Quantity: 300*f*
Title, Whence Derived: Spanish
Title Dated: 26 April 1790
Remarks: **Prosper King** says, "that John Montgomery was the head of a family at the date of the warrant and the claimant made a small improvement on the premises in the year 1798." [Footnote:] The act of Congress, passed on the 3d of March, 1823, "For the relief of the heirs and representatives of Alexander Montgomery, deceased," authorizes them to locae other lands in lieu of those contained in this order of survey.

Register's No.: 577
Present Claimant: **James Williams**
Original Claimant: **Henry Willis**
Situation: Bayou Sara
Quantity: 800*f*
Title, Whence Derived: Spanish
Title Dated: 23 May 1791
Remarks: See under Register's Number 578 which follows.

Register's No.: 578
Present Claimant: **James Williams**
Original Claimant: **James Sanders**
Situation: Bayou Sara
Quantity: 500*f*
Title, Whence Derived: Spanish
Title Dated: Quantity: 5 July 1789
Remarks: The and was sold by Sanders to **Henry Willis** in 1791; and Willis, on the 2nd September 1794, devised these two tracts, with others, to his wife, now **Sarah F. Chotard**, arid his son **Lewis Willis,** who died; whereupon, his mother became possessed of his part of the property, who, together with her husband, **John Chotard La Place**, conveyed by deed to the claimant, 1st September 1803. **William McIntosh** says, "that Henry Willis, in the year

1792, was an actual settler in the Mississippi territory, who left the country, with the permission of the Spanish Government, on necessary business, with the intention of returning; that Willis and Sanders (the original warantees) were heads of families at the date of the warrant." **Mary Connor** says, "that **Henry Willis,** when he went to the State of Georgia, about the year 1794, left papers of considerable value, and also horses and cattle, his right to which has not been disputed by any person, in the possession of Mrs. **Ann Savage,** who also paid several debts for the said Willis during his absence; and further saith, that when she was in Georgia, in the year 1796, and in the neighborhood in which Willis resided after he left the country, also understood that he prepared to return to this country as soon as he could go to Charleston, in South Carolina, and return; at which place, she understood, he died in the year 1794." **Abram Ellis** says, "that shortly before Henry Willis left this country to go to Georiga, having a note of said Willis's, applied to him for payment, and was informed by him that Mrs. Savage would pay it for him, and that she was to attend to his business during his absence; and also, that the said Willis informed him that he intended to return to this country." **William Conner** says, "that all the patents of the lands in the Mississippi territory, of Henry Willis, deceased, now claimed by **James Williams,** as purchaser under the said Henry Willis, were among the papers of Mrs. Savage when her papers came into the hands of the witness, in the year 1798; also several other papers of the said Henry Willis, which showed that Mrs. Savage paid large sums of money towards the consideration money of the said lands during the absence of the said Henry Willis from this territory."

Register's No.: 581
Present Claimant: **Peter Presler**
Original Claimant: **John O'Connor**
Situation: Cole's creek
Quantity: 400*f*
Title, Whence Derived: Spanish
Title Dated: 26 April 1790
Remarks: No evidence.

Register's No.: 586
Present Claimant: **John Foster**
Original Claimant: **Elias Bonnell**
Situation: River Homochitto
Quantity: 152*f*
Title, Whence Derived: Spanish
Title Dated: Quantity: May 1790
Remarks: **William Atchison** says, "that Elias Bonnell was upwards of twenty-one years of age at the date of the warrant, and that he, the witness, surveyed the land in question about the year 1791."

INDEX

Alston, John, 19
Alston, Phillip, 18
Alston, Solomon, 19
Amoss, Adam, 3
Amoss, James, 3
Amoss, James, 5
Amoss, James, 16
Armstreet, John, 21
Atchison, William, 40
Baker, John, 23
Baker, John, 26
Barbour, James, 12
Barbour, James, 18
Barbour, James, 20
Barbut, James, 27
Barland, William, 34
Barnet, Daniel, 38
Barry, Richard, 16
Bassett, Thomas, 22
Bassett, Thomas, 26
Bay, Elihu Hall, 11
Bay, Elihu Hall, 12
Bay, Elihu Hall, 23
Bay, Elihu Hall, 24
Bay, Elihu Hall, 27
Bay, William, 10
Bay, William, 12
Bernard, J.[oseph], heirs of, 35
Bernard, Joseph, 35
Biggs, William, 6
Blommart, John, 16
Bonnell, Elias, 40
Bowrne, John Frederick, 3
Bradley, John, 2
Bremarr, Francis, 13
Bremarr, F., 27
Brocksopp, C., 5
Brocksopp, Edward, 3
Burdon, George, 24
Burling, Thomas, 30
Burr, A., Vice President of the United States, 5
Callender, Robert, 16
Caller, James, 25

Canning, --, 1
Canning, George, Secretary of State, 4
Carr, Ann, 18
Cartwright, Peter, 22
Cassiter, Charles, 23
Chambers, Joseph, Board of Commissioners, 26
Chennery, Broderick, Sir, 5
Chesta, W., Major, 5
Chotard La Place, John, 39
Chotard, Sarah F., 39
Clark, George Rogers, General, 6
Clark, Daniel, 8
Clark, Daniel, 9
Clark, William, 25
Clark, William, 25
Clark, William, 28
Clarke, Arthur, 2
Clarke, Arthur, 5
Cloyd, Robert, heirs of, 34
Cloyd, Robert, 34
Cloyd, Robert, 35
Cochran, --, 18
Cochran, Robert, 33
Coleman, Francis, 22
Coleman, Francis, 26
Collins, Luke, surveyor, 37
Collins, William, 15
Comyn, Thomas, 5
Comyn, Thomas, 5
Conner, William, 40
Connor, Mary, 40
Connor. See also O'Connor
Conway, Maurice, 33
Conway, William, 33
Corey, David, 37
Corey, Job, 36
Cox, Tench, 20
Crane, Waterman, 37
Crozier, Richard, 37
Cushing, Elijah, 19
Dalzel, Archibald, 2
Dalzel, Archibald, 5
Davy, Thomas, 26
Davy, Thomas, 27
De Forge, Peter, 23

Dickson, David, 27
Dorsey, Benjamin, 35
Dow, Lorenzo, 21
Dunbar, William, 33
Dunbar, William, district surveyor, 38
Durham, Thomas, 16
Eglinton, Earl of, 29
Ellis, Abram, 40
Erskine, D. M., 1
Evan, Edward, 20
Evans, Edward, 31
Evans, Thomas, 35
Falconer, John, 3
Falling, William Wingdam, 5
Fanning, James, 17
Fanning, Sylvester, 17
Farmer, Robert, 16
Farmer, Robert, 22
Farmer, Robert, 23
Farrar, Benjamin, 20
Ferguson, James, 20
Ferguson, John, Admiral, 5
Firby, John, 18
Forge, De. See De Forge
Fortner, T., 38
Fortner, V., 38
Foster, John, 40
Foster, Thomas, 36
Fradgely, William, 24
Frere, George, 5
Fricker, William, 13
Fricker, William, 18
Fricker, William, 28
Fry, Thomas, 18
Gallagher, Jacintha, 32
Gallatin, Albert, 7
Gallatin, Albert, Esq., Secretary of the Treasury, 26
Garnier, William, 5
Garnier, William, 11
Garnier, William, 21
Garvey, Henry, 32
Garvey, Henry, 32
Gasling, --, Captain, 2
Gayoso, --, Governor, 38
Germain, Jeremiah, 15

Gibson, Reuben, 36
Gilliard, Theodore, 23
Godley, William, 3
Godley, William, 18
Goldfinch, Henry, 5
Gordon, Adam, 5
Graham, Colin, Esq., 7
Grant, Allen, 23
Grant, William, 11
Grant, William, 13
Green, Rawleigh, 22
Green, Thomas, 33
Green, Thomas M., 33
Green, Thomas M., 34
Green, Everard, 35
Green, Thomas M., 36
Guice, Christopher, 9
Guice, Christopher, 10
Halderman, Anthony Francis, 28
Halderman, Anthony Francis, 29
Halderman, Frederick, 28
Halderman, Frederick, 29
Haldermand, Frederick, 17
Hamilton, Cyrus, 35
Harcourt, --, General, 5
Hardy, Thomas, 19
Harman, Jacob, 36
Hodge, David, 16
Hodge, David, 17
Hoggatt, James, 25
Hoggatt, James, 26
Holliday, Samuel, 21
Hooper, James, 7
Hooper, Absalom, 19
Hughes, James, 14
Hughes, Daniel, 20
Hunt, Abijah, 31
Hunt, Abijah, 32
Hutchins, Thomas, 18
Hutchins, Thomas, Junior, 21
Hutchins, Thomas, Senior, 21
Hutson, Noah Kenner, 25
Jackson, Joseph, 21
Jacobs, Susanna, 14
James, Thomas, 14

Jefferson, James, 5
Jefferson, Thomas, 5
Johnson, --, General, 3
Johnson, William, 20
Johnson, Daniel, 25
Johnson, William, 28
Johnston, John, 24
Jones, James, 20
Kelly, Patrick, 13
Kemplin, Nicholas, 33
King, Joseph, 20
King, Joseph, 36
King, Prosper, 37
King, Prosper, 37
King, Prosper, 38
King, Prosper, 39
King, Richard, Dragoon commander, 38
Konovan, --, 5
La Place. See Chotard La Place
Lanehart, Adam, 39
Lawrence, Ann, 22
Lawrence, Ann, 24
Lehnhardt. See Lanehart
Lewis, William, 32
Little, Abraham, 22
Lloyd, Joseph W. A., 18
Lloyd, J. A. W., 27
Lorimer, Catherine, 5
Lorimer, John, Doctor, 11
Lorimer, K., 2
Lott, John, Junior, 25
Lyman, Thaddeus, 12
Lyman, Thaddeus, 20
Lyman, Thaddeus, 20
Lyman, Thaddeus, 29
MacDonald, Alexander, Major, 3
Macon, Nathaniel, Speaker of House of Representatives, 5
Macullagh, Alexander, 13
Macullagh, Alexander, 25
Macullagh, A., 28
Madison, James, 1
Madison, James, 3
Madison, James, Honorable, 5
Malone, Peter, 23
Marshall, William, 13

Marshall, William, 21
Marshall, William, 27
Matthews, Hugh, 39
McCaleb, John, 29
McCaleb, William, 13
McCaleb, William, 27
McCoy, John, 37
McDonald, Alexander, 5
McGillivray, John, 2
McGillivray, James, 2
McGillivrayers, John, 5
McGrew, Clark, 22
McGrew, John, Esq., 22
McGrew, John, Senior, 22
McGrew, John, Esq., 26
McGrew, John, Senior, 26
McIntosh, Alexander, 17
McIntosh, John, 22
McIntosh, William, 39
McKennon, William, 5
Merry, Anthony, 4
Merry, Anthony, 5
Miller, John, 3
Miller, John, 3
Miller, John, 5
Mills, William, 16
Mims, Samuel, 25
Minor, Stephen, 34
Minor, Stephen, 38
Moira, Earl of, 5
Montgomeril, --, 5
Montgomery, Alexander, 37
Montgomery, Alexander, 37
Montgomery, Alexander, 38
Montgomery, Alexander, 39
Montgomery, John, 39
Moore, James, 30
Moore, James, 30
Moore, James, 31
Moore, James, 31
Moore, Maria, 30
Moore, Moses, 22
Moore, Moses, 24
Moore, Robert, 30
Moore, Robert, 31

Moore, Robert, 31
Moore, Samuel P., 31
Moore, Samuel P., 31
Moore, William, 31
Morrow, Jeremiah, 6
Neil, Eleanor, 5
Neil, J. T., 5
Nicholas, Robert C., Board of Commissioners, 26
Nunn, John, 5
O'Connor, John, 40
Ogden, Amos, Captain, 7
Ogden, Amos, 12
Ogden, Amos, 19
Ogden, Amos, 20
Ogdon, Amos, 21
Ogden, John, 19
Ogden, Jonathan, 2
Ogilvy, William, 3
Page, John, 5
Paul --, Captain, 5
Pearne, Richard Freeman, 17
Peck, John, 29
Person, Harrison, 35
Peterkin, James, 28
Peters, John, 38
Pickering, John, 22
Piernas, Peter, Esq., 33
Piernas, Peter, Lieutenant Governor, 34
Pollock, Oliver, 15
Presler, Peter, 40
Prevost, Augustine, 15
Prevost, G., Sir Major General, Baronet, 5
Prevost, James Marcus, 12
Prevost, James M., 13
Rain, Cornelius, 24
Ramsey, James, 16
Ransford, Andrew, 17
Rhea, --, 18
Ridgeley, Nicholas G., 31
Roberts, Charles, 3
Roberts, Charles, 5
Rodney, Thomas, Board of Commissioners, 7
Rodney, George Brydges, Sir, 20
Ryan, Daniel, 28
Ryan, Winifred, 35

Sanders, James, 39
Savage, Ann, 40
Schilling, Palser, 34
Scott, John, 14
Scott, Sarah, 31
Scott, William, 31
Shaw, Charles, 2
Shaw, Charles, 5
Shaw, Charles, 5
Shaw, John, Major, 2
Shaw, --, Lieutenant General, 2
Shaw, --, Lieutenant General, 5
Shearl, J., Major General, 5
Small, --, Major General, 5
Smith, John, 11
Sommers, John, 17
Southwell, John, 13
Southwell, John, 13
Stampley, John, 39
Stephenson, J., 2
Stephenson, John, 14
Steuart, James, 38
Strother, Arthur, 3
Strother, Thomas, 3
Struther, Ar[thur?], 5
Struthey, William, 2
Stuart, --, Major General, 2
Stuart, Charles Swede, 2
Stuart, Charles, 5
Sulteney, William, 2
Sutherland, John, 23
Swanson, Peter, 2
Swanson, Peter, 3
Swanson, Peter, 5
Swanson, Peter, 5
Swanson, Peter, 5
Taitt, David, 5
Taitt, Richard, 5
Taylor, Abraham, 36
Thompson, Margaret, 32
Thompson, Thomas, 32
Thornell, Ephraim, 19
Todd, Edward, 17
Trudeau, Charles, Surveyor General, 34
Truly, Bennet, 35

Turnbull, Robert J., 12
Vardiman, William, 25
Varlo, George, 5
Varlo, Weston, 26
Varlo, Weston, 27
Vidal, Jacintha, 32
Vousdan, William, 30
Wadsworth, Thomas, 21
Wailes, Edward, Lieutenant, 23
Walker, Charles, 26
Wall, William, 25
Wallis, Catura, 34
Ward, Daniel, 17
Ward, Daniel, 18
Ward, Daniel, 28
Ward, Joshua, 18
Waugh, David, 19
Wells, Robert, 5
Wells, William Charles, 5
Westmoreland, Joseph, 22
White, James, 31
White, James, 31
White, James, 31
Whitley, Solomon, 37
Whittle, Maria, 30
William, Robert, Board of Commissioners, 7
Williams, James, 39
Williams, James, 39
Williams, James, 40
Williams, Thomas H., Board of Commissioners, 7
Williams, Thomas H., Register of Land Office, 29
Willis, Henry, 39
Willis, Henry, 39
Willis, Henry, 40
Willis, Lewis, 39
Willis, Sarah F., 39
Wilton, William, 27
Wilton, William, 28
Winfree, Jacob, 19

Selections from **The American State Papers**
Monograph Number 6

SPANISH AND BRITISH LAND GRANTS

IN MISSISSIPPI TERRITORY, 1750-1784

CLIFFORD NEAL SMITH

First printing, September 1996   rz

FOREWORD

The American State Papers are official public documents printed privately long before the Congressional Printing Office existed. The printing of public documents during the very early Congresses was done without any general provision of law as to what should be printed. Even as early as 1829 the clerk of the House of Representatives reported that, for the period 1793-1803 not a vestige of manuscript and only a scattered few printed copies were extant. A contributing factor was the destruction of the Capitol building in 1814 by fire.

In 1821 a bill was passed which authorized the publication of 750 copies of all the documents that could be found. The documents were published by two private companies: Gales and Seaton, and Duff Green. Of the two publications, Gales and Seaton is the larger. The Duff Green collection of documents are less comprehensive than the Gales and Seaton collection, and there are many differences in the pagination, particularly in later volumes.

Both publishers appear to have divided the original documents into general subject categories: Foreign Affairs, Indian Affairs, Finance, Commerce and Navigation, Military Affairs, Naval Affairs, Post Office Department, Public Land, and Claim. For genealogical and family history researchers, the last two categories--Public Land and Claims--are the most valuable, and it is from these two categories that this monograph *Selections from* **The American State Papers** will be made. The Public Land category, in eight volumes, covers the period 1789-1837; the Claims category, in one volume, covers the period 1790-1823.

In 1972 an attempt was made to index all names in the Public Land and Claims categories of the American State Papers; the index, although monumental, is, however, not complete. All researchers are urged to read pages i through xxvii of

Phillip McMullin, editor, *Grassroots of America: A Computerized Index to the American State Papers: Land Grants and Claims (1789-1837) with Other Aids to Research* (Salt Lake City, Utah: Gendex Corporation, 1972).

The present *Selections from the American State Papers* are the selections, by narrower subject matter, from the Gales and Seaton edition, made by this compiler for the use of genealogists and family historians because the original volumes are now very rare and, no doubt, inaccessible to most researchers.

(ASP 8:1:613)

D. (continued)

Report of Claims founded on British and Spanish Warrants of Survey within the District west of Pearl River, disallowed by the Board of Commissioners, made in pursuance of the fourth section of an act, entitled "An act concerning the sales of the lands of the United States and for other purposes," passed 31 March 1808.

Register's No.: 625
Present Claimant: **George Cochran,** heirs of
Original Claimant: **George Cochran**
Situation: Bayou Pierre
Quantity: 200*f*
Title, Whence Derived: Spanish
Title Dated: 18 January 1793
Remarks: No evidence

Register's No.: 624
Present Claimant: **George Cochran**, heirs of
Original Claimant: **Martin Carney**
Situation: Cole's creek
Quantity: 240*f*
Title, Whence Derived: Spanish
Title Dated: 30 October 1790
Remarks: **William Thomas** says, "that Martin Carney was twenty-one years of age at the date of the warrant, and inhabited the land before and at the date of the warrant, by living in a house he had built, but never cultivated it, and then sold it to the claimant, and there has never been any cultivation or habitation of it since Carney sold it." (13th March 1797).

Register's No.: 690
Present Claimant: **Henry Roach**
Original Claimant: **Henry Roach**
Situation: Buffalo creek
Quantity: 1,038*f*
Title, Whence Derived: Spanish
Title Dated: --
Remarks: No order of survey has been produced, and the only evidence that such a document ever existed is contained in a certificate signed in 1803 by **William Atchison,** formerly a deputy surveyor, stating, in substance, that he had surveyed the land in question for the claimant by virtue of an order from **Manuel Gayoso,** in 1793, (who was then the Governor of the district), that every person should enjoy the swamp in front of their land. **William Roach**

says, "that the land in question is swmp land, on the Buffalo creek, near the mouth, and that the claimant lived on bluff land adjoinint it in the year 1787, and for twelve or fourteen years following; during the whole time the claimant got boards, shingles, and rails off the premises in question; no other use was ever made of it, except for getting timber."

(ASP 8:1:614)

Register's No.: 711
Present Claimant: **P. King** and **R. King**
Original Claimant: **Justus King**
Situation: Homochitto river
Quantity: 500
Title, Whence Derived: British
Title Dated: --
Remarks: No order of survey produced. **Caleb King** says, "that he believes that Justus King, deceased, who was his brother, had a British warrant for five hundred acres, and he believes he surveyed the land in question under the said warrant, but it has never been settled or improved. After the land was surveyed, Justus King was driven away from that part of the country by an Indian war, but resided in the territory until he died, and was the head of a family at the date of the warrant." **Nathan Swayze** says, "that he was present at the surveying of the land in question by one **Samuel Lewis**, a lawful surveyor under the British Government, in the year 1776, but it never was inhabited or cultivated, owing to danger from the Indians, who drove off people from that part of the country; but that Justus King lived in the territory until he died, which was about six years ago." (1798).

Register's No.: 712
Present Claimant: **Stephen Swayze**
Original Claimant: **Stephen Swayze**
Situation: Homochitto river
Quantity: 500
Title, Whence Derived: British
Title Dated: --
Remarks: No warrant produced, nor any other evidence offered in support of [this] claim.

Register's No.: 713
Present Claimant: **Nathan Swayze**
Original Claimant: **Samuel Swayze**
Situation: Homochitto river
Quantity: 500
Title, Whence Derived: British
Title Dated: --
Remarks: No warrant produced, nor any other evidence offered in support of [this] claim.

Register's No.: 739
Present Claimant: **Nehemiah Carter**
Original Claimant: **Nehemiah Carter**
Situation: Boyd's creek
Quantity: 1,200
Title, Whence Derived: British
Title Dated: 21 November 1798
Remarks: **John Gaskins** says, "that the claimant resided in the Mississippi territory on the 27th October 1795, and was above twenty-one years of age at the date of the warrant." **Anthony Hutchins** says, "that the claimant was an inhabitant of the Mississippi territory at the date of the warrant of survey, and has continued to be so ever since."

Register's No.: 739
Present Claimant: **John Henderson**
Original Claimant: **William Henderson**
Situation: Thompson's creek
Quantity: 1,000*f*
Title, Whence Derived: British
Title Dated: 16 March 1777
Remarks: **John Boil** says, "that William Henderson was twenty-one years of age at the date of the warrant and that the claimant was an actual settler in the Mississippi territory before the 27th of October, 1795, and has been ever since but the premises have not been inhabited or cultivated."

Register's No.: 746
Present Claimant: **Charles Boardman,** heirs of
Original Claimant: **Charles Boardman**
Situation: Fairchild's creek
Quantity: 226*f*
Title, Whence Derived: Spanish
Title Dated: --
Remarks: No order of survey produced; but a certificate from **William Atchison,** without date, stating "that he had surveyed the same by an order from **Charles Trudeau** to **William Dunbar.**"

Register's No.: 747
Present Claimant: **Charles Boardman,** heirs of
Original Claimant: **Charles Boardman**
Situation: Fairchild's creek
Quantity: 282*f*
Title, Whence Derived: Spanish
Title Dated: --
Remarks: No warrant produced, nor any other evidence, except "an order from the Surveyor General of the Spanish Government, direct to **William Dunbar,** requesting him to survey the land between Boardman's claim and Fairchild's creek, daed 19th November 1791; also, a

certificate from William Dunbar, that he had surveyed the land in favor of Charles Boardman, dated 2d June 1793."

Register's No.: 752
Present Claimant: **Isaac Gaillard**
Original Claimant: **John McCoy***
Situation: Homochitto river
Quantity: 300*f*
Title, Whence Derived: Spanish
Title Dated: 28 March 1794
Remarks: **Alexander McKay** says, "that John McKay*, the patentee, was the head of a family at the date of the warrant' and the witness helped him to build a cabin on the premises in the year 1796; and they completed it, and cut down cane and saplings on a small spot of ground where the house stood, and then the witness went away, and knows nothing further about the place."
[*so spelled]

Register's No.: 766
Present Claimant: **Garret Rapalje**, heirs of
Original Claimant: **Garret Rapalje**
Situation: River Mississippi
Quantity: 1,000*f*
Title, Whence Derived: Spanish
Title Dated: 26 April 1790
Remarks: **John Shackler** says, "that in 1791 he went up with Governor **[Manuel] Gayoso** to the Walnut Hills when he went to settle a garrison there, when he saw an old field adjoining the Rapalje Bayou and the Mississippi, below the bayou aforesaid; on which field there was then a cabin uninhabited; there was some ground on the field broken up, and looked like potato hills, as if potatoes had been planted there; that he understood by the Governor and Col. **[John] Girault**, that Garret Rapalje built the cabin, but said that he should not have it. The witness has seen Garret Rapalje often at the Walnut hills; has heard him say the settlement aforesaid was his, and he should try to get it, but never saw him exercise any ownership on the premises now claimed; some years afterward

(ASP 8:1:615)

he heard from others that Garret Rapalje was gone to the States for his family, and died there; and he knows four of his sons, to wit, **George [Rapalje], Isaac [Rapalje], Jacques [Rapalje]** and **Garret [Rapalje, Junior]**; Jacques was in this country in the year 1789, and continued here until he died in 1797; George came in 1796, and this has been his place of residence ever since; Isaac was here, and several times back and forward to the Walnut hills before his father, Garret, went away; Garret, the younger, has lived, and does live, below the line. The heirs aforesaid have never been in possessionof the premises claimed that the witness knows of." **John Girault** a witness introduced by **Elihu Hall Bay**, a conflicting claimant, says, "that, early in the year 1791, he attended Governor Gayoso on a visit to the Walnut hills, to view the place where the Governor intended to erect a fortification; that, on their arrival at Watkin's creek, they found a small cabin on the lower side of it, where they encamped all night; after the Governor [**Manuel Gayoso**] had been informed that the cabin was erected by **Garret Rapalje,** he appeared surprised that Rapalje should have persisted in erecting it after being forbidden by him; the Governor then took posssssion of it in the name of the [Spanish] King, and wrote on one side of the joists, 'Casa Gayoso'; there was no person at or about the place, nor any appearance of recent cultivation, but there was an old field which the witness took to be the settlement of -- **Watkins,** as he, the witness, had been there in 1775, and, from information understood that Watkins lived there at that time. In the latter part of the month of March following, the Governor returned to erect the fortification he had before proposed, and, on the 1st of April, arrived at the same cabin which was still uninhabited, and stopped and dined there; that a number of artificers were present for the purpose of erecting the fort, among whom was **John Shackler**. Aftewards Rapalje made application to permit him to return and inhabit the house, which the Governor positively refused; the witness knows that several other applications were made to settle the Walnut hills, which were also refused; the witness was frequently at the Waltnut hills afterwards, and never saw Rapalje, or any of his family, inhabiting or cultivating the tenement; but the witness does not know, of his own knowledge, whether Rapalje cultivated the premises or not, but rather things he did not."

Register's No.: 777
Present Claimant: **Jos[eph] W. A. Lloyd**
Original Claimant: **William Vardiman**
Situation: Wills's creek
Quantity: 500*f*
Title, Whence Derived: Spanish
Title Dated: 28 September 1794
Remarks: **Joshua Howard** says, "that William Vardiman was a resident in the Mississippi territory on the 27th October 1795, and was twenty-one years of age at the date of the warrant."

Register's No.: 778
Present Claimant: **Jos[eph] W. A. Lloyd**
Original Claimant: **Anthony Calvit**
Situation: Homochitto river
Quantity: 200*f*
Title, Whence Derived: Spanish
Title Dated: 18 January 1793
Remarks: No evidence

Register's No.: 787
Present Claimant: **Thomas Percy**
Original Claimant: **Thomas Percy**
Situation: Bayou Sara
Quantity: 800*f*
Title, Whence Derived: Spanish
Title Dated: 11 April 1789

Remarks: **John Collins** says, "that the claimant was a resident in the Mississippi territory on the 27th October 1795."

Register's No.: 809
Present Claimant: **John Ellis**
Original Claimant: **Thomas Green**
Situation: Thompson's creek
Quantity: 800*f*
Title, Whence Derived: Spanish
Title Dated: 24 February 1795
Remarks: **Bennet Truly** says, "that Thomas Green was an actual settler in the Mississippi territory on the 27th October 1795, and that he was then the head of a family." **Ferdinand L. Claiborne** says, "that he paid for the claimant, Colonel **John Ellis,** to Colonel Thomas Green, two thousand dollars, being the consideration money for a tract of land lying on the bayou Sara, which the said John Ellis had purchased of the said Green, which tract contained eight hundred arpents."

Register's No.: 810
Present Claimant: **Robert Dunbar**
Original Claimant: **Francis Jones**
Situation: Cole's creek
Quantity: 400*f*
Title, Whence Derived: Spanish
Title Dated: 6 June 1790
Remarks: **John Roberts** says, "that Francis Jones came into the country in the year 1788, to look for land, and procured a warrant of survey from the Spanish Government, and left it in the hands of **Henry Green**, to have it laid and surveyed, who did the same on the land now claimed; in the meantime, to wit, in the fall of 1788, Jones went to the States to fetch his family, and brought them to the neighborhood, and went on the land with his negroes in May, 1798, and began improving, and cleared trees and cane off of about four or five acres, and prepared timber for a house, and then sold it to -- Ferguson, -- Wooley & Co. who sold to the claimant." Henry Green's deposition, "I do certify, that, in the year 1789, to the best of my recollection, Francis Jones petitioned the Spanish Government for a certain tract of land, containing four hundred arpents, joining the land I now cultivate; the abovementioned tract was granted to the said Jones, and surveyed by my direction in the year 1791, as agent for Mr. Jones, and kept in possession for said Jones by me, as his agent, until 1798, when said Jones removed to the country, took possession, and improved, and planted fruit trees on said tract." **William Thomas** says, "that the premises in question were improved either in the year 1790 or 1791, but the witness does not recollect by whom, nor whether the improvement was continued, and having been that way since."

(ASP 8:1:616)

7

Register's No.: 813
Present Claimant: **Robert Dunbar**
Original Claimant: **Robert Dunbar**
Situation: Bayou Pierre
Quantity: 250
Title, Whence Derived: British
Title Dated: 12 February 1778
Remarks: **Benjamin Bealk** says, "that the claimant was an actual settler, and the head of a family, in the Mississippi territory, in the year 1781, to the best of his knowledge and belief, and was previous to that time." **James Truly** says, "that Robert Dunbar was an actual settler in the Mississippi territory on said and before the date of the warrant, to wit, on the 12th February, 1788, and was then the head of a family; that the said order of survey did not come to the hands of the said Robert [Dunbar], in consequence, as he believes, of the war which prevailed at that time between the British and Spanish Governments, until about the summer of 1803, when it was found among the papers of one **Richard Harrison**, after his death; said Dunbar being entitled to so much land, as a head right, under the British Government and expecting a confirmation of his title, disposed of it to said Harrison, and gave his obligation to said Harrison to confirm the same to him when the titles should be fully completed. That deponent further says, that one **Philip Barber,** the uncle and co-partner in trade of the said Harrison, was taken by the Spaniards on his way from Pensacola to this country, about the year 1778, and, with his papers, was carried to New Orleans; and that this deponent believes the above mentioned warrant of survey to have been among them, as he this deponent, afterwards found it in a trunk of the said Harrison, after his death, with other papers of a like description.

Register's No.: 882
Present Claimant: **John Crunkleton**
Original Claimant: **James Crunkleton**
Situation: Bayou Pierre
Quantity: 640
Title, Whence Derived: British
Title Dated: --
Remarks: No warrant produced. **Patrick Cogan** says, "he has been acquainted fourteen years with the land in question, and seven years with the claimant. The land, when he was first acquainted with it, appeared to have been formerly settled by some person; and he understood, in the neighborhood, that it belonged to the father of the claimant, and that he formerly resided on it . He understood, also, that the father left the country on account of war in it between the Indians and Spaniards, or at least on account of public troubles." **Zachariah Kirkland** says, "that about two years ago the claimant came to him and offered him lands for sale on James's creek, which he believes to be the land now claimed; that the claimant then showed him a part of a British warrant granted to his father, the other part being lost, but knows not what land it was for; that he heard **John Staybraker** say, that he had been at the house of the claimant's father, when he lived upon the land in question." **Joseph Dyson** says, "that a certain **Thomas Jones** went to Pensacola, in the year 1778, to get a warrant for **James Symmons**, and another for James Crunkleton, the father of the claimant; and, after said Thomas Jones returned, he saw the warrant in Crunkleton's hands, which he understood was for the land in question, and that Crunkleton

settled on the land immediately, and cultivated it for about two years, and then went to the States on account of the rebellion here. In about three or four years **[James] Crunkleton** returned with an intention to settle on the land again, but was taken sick and died. The present claimant, immediately after he got married, settled on the land in question, as the witness believes, and has continued to inhabit and cultivate the same ever since; that it is the same place his father formerly settled on as before mentioned, and there are about six acres or more cleared, and a dwelling house and out-houses." On cross-examination, he does not know what quantity of land the warrant called for.

Register's No.: 888
Present Claimant: **George Matthews**
Original Claimant: **Adam Cloud**
Situation: Bayou Sara
Quantity: 1,000*f*
Title, Whence Derived: Spanish
Title Dated: --
Remarks: No warrant produced. Stated to be lost.

(ASP 8:1:617)

Register's No.: 889
Present Claimant: **George Matthews**
Original Claimant: **Adam Cloud**
Situation: Cole's creek
Quantity: 500*f*
Title, Whence Derived: Spanish
Title Dated: 30 March 1790
Remarks: **John Girault** says, "that Adam Cloud moved on the land with his family in the year 1789, or 1790, and cultivated it for two or three years following, and then moved off. The witness does not know whether Adam Cloud resided in the Mississippi territory on the 27th October 1795. Cloud was sent out of the territory by order of the Spanish Government, and left Colonel -- **Forman** as his attorney."

Register's No.: 824
Present Claimant: **William Clare**
Original Claimant: **William Clare**
Situation: Cole's creek
Quantity: 240*f*
Title, Whence Derived: Spanish
Title Dated: --
Remarks: No warrant produced; but a survey made by **William Thomas,** dated 20th February 1795, by an order of **William Dunbar**, dated 13 February 1795. **Henry Stampley** says. "that the claimant was about twenty years of age at the date of the survey. About four years ago,

(1801) the claimant cleared and cultivated about six acres, and made crop on it, and has done nothing since that the witness knows of."

Register's No.: 937
Present Claimant: **Catherine Surget**
Original Claimant: **Peter Surget**
Situation: Feliciana creek
Quantity: 800*f*
Title, Whence Derived: Spanish
Title Dated: 13 November 1794
Remarks: **William Atchison** says, "that Peter Surget and **Charles Surget** severally inhabited and cultivate the tracts on the 27th October 1795, and that the former was the head of a family, and the latter twenty-one years of age at the date of the warrant." **Samuel Stockett** says, "that in the year 1802, in the month of March, he came to this country for the purpose of settling, and intended doing so on vacant land, by which intention he had occasion to travel over the land claimed as above stated, and that there was no settlement, or appearance of cultivation, on any part of the above tract; after which, he, this deponent, returned to the State of Tennessee, and came back in the fall following 1802, and traversed said tracts, with other lands, and still discovered no settlement on the said tract; but in consequence of seeing some old marked lines, he did not settle on said lands." **Isaac Johnson** says, "that he is well acquainted with the land in question (to wit: No. 1372), that he came to this country in the year 1800, and that he went over this tract, and another tract adjoining to, and belonging to the brother of the claimant (to wit: No. 937,) with an intention of purchasing. In the year 1800, at the time he called on Mr. Surget to make a purchase of it; Mr. Surget informed him that a part of the lands, containing thirteen hundred acres, belonging to him, and a part to his brother; that those two tracts were in one survey, one of eight hundred arpents, and the other of five hundred arpents, but that there were two rights for them. On his return to this country, in the year 1801, he went over these two tracts, and observed the lines, and three or four corner trees marked with the name of Surget, that he traveled over the greater part, if not all the lands in these two tracts in the spring of 1801, and that there was not then the least evidence of any improvement or cultivation, as the witness observed, on either of the tracts." **Moses Starnes** says, "that he is acquainted with the premises in question, as he has been frequently over them. In February, 1801, he moved to this country, and settled within a mile or a mile and a half of the premises. He very often traveled over the tract of five hundred arpents, and another tract adjoining thereto, which was claimed by the Surgets, and which he understood were all one claim; that he believes there are not one hundred square yards of both these tracts that he has not traveled over. At the time this deponent first went over these tracts of land, in March 1801, and to the present day, he never discovered the least evidence of an improvement or cultivation on either of the tracts. The only evidence which he discovered, was some marked corner trees, which marks appeared not to be more than two or three years standing." **William Atchison,** the evidence whose testimony has been previously stated in these claims, being present before the Board, disavows the evidence formerly given, and says that the lands were never inhabited or cultivated as heretofore stated.

Register's No.: 1327
Present Claimant: **Charles Surget**
Original Claimant: **Charles Surget**
Situation: Feliciana creek
Quantity: 500*f*
Title, Whence Derived: Spanish
Title Dated: 13 December 1794
Remarks: [See Register's No. 937 immediately above]

Register's No.: 958
Present Claimant: **Ann Brashears**
Original Claimant: **Ann Brashears**
Situation: Bayou Pierre
Quantity: 300*f*
Title, Whence Derived: Spanish
Title Dated: --
Remarks: No warrant was produced, but a certificate by **William Vousdan** that a survey was made on the 11th November 1788. **William Thomas** says, "that the claimant obtained a warrant from the Spanish Government for eight hundred arpents, upwards of fourteen years ago; that the witness acted as deputy surveyor to William Vousdan, who was surveyor for this district at the time; and, in virtue of said warrant or order, surveyed a tract of land of eight hundred arpents, on the north side of the north fork of the Bayou Pierre, which survey included a place called the White Ground Like, near to which a certain **Benjamin Foy** resided in what is called a camp, near the centre of the land; that the present claim of three hundred arpents is included in the

(ASP 8:1:618)

survey of eight hundred arpents before mentioned; and the witness knows nothing further of the claim, nor why Vousdan did not return the whole survey." **John Girault** says, "that, after William Vousdan resigned, **William Dunbar** was appointed the surveyor of Natchez district by the Spanish Government, and that he, the witness, acting as deputy surveyor under him, surveyed a tract of land, by order of the Spanish Government, of three hundred and twenty arpents, for the above mentioned Benjamin Foy, within the survey of eight hundred arpents aforesaid; that the said Foy, being interpreter to the Spanish Government, was favored by them, and had a grant for five hundred arpents, as the witness understood; but, as Mrs. Brashears had a prior right, he agreed to take only three hundred and twenty arpents out of the eight hundred arpents aforesaid, which the witness surveyed for him as aforesaid, and left the residue for Mrs. Brashears; that said survey was made on the upper end of said eight hundred acre tract." Major **Stephen Minor** says. "that he, the witness, knows that a warrant of survey issued from the Spanish Government to the claimant for eight hundred arpents, about fourteen or fifteen years ago." (1790).

Register's No.: 965
Present Claimant: **Isaac Johnson**
Original Claimant: **Jemima Morgan**
Situation: Cole's creek

Quantity: 350
Title, Whence Derived: British
Title Dated: --
Remarks: No warrant produced. **Robert Miller** says, "that a small improvement or clearing was made on the premises by the hands of **William Erwine** in 1795, and Jemima Morgan was of age in 1779."

Register's No.: 972
Present Claimant: **John Holt**
Original Claimant: **Joseph Sharp**
Situation: Cole's creek
Quantity: 640*f*
Title, Whence Derived: Spanish
Title Dated: --
Remarks: The only evidence produced is a petition by Joseph Sharp for six hundred arpents, dated 17th November 1795, which appears not to have been presented to the Spanish Government, as there is no decree on it. There is also a plot and survey, made in September 1796, by **Silas L. Paine,** but no authority mentioned by which it was done.

Register's No.: 1001
Present Claimant: **John Ellis**
Original Claimant: **William Wikoff**
Situation: Bayou Sara
Quantity: 800*f*
Title, Whence Derived: Spanish
Title Dated: 15 April 1789
Remarks: **William Atchison** says, "that he surveyed the land in question for the claimant by the request of William Wikoff, who said he had sold it to the claimant; and the witness says that Wikoff was of age at the date of the warrant, and the land was not at that time inhabited or cultivated, and has not been so since that he knows of.

Register's No.: 1090
Present Claimant: **A. Hunt** and **W. G. Forman**
Original Claimant: **Richard Devall**
Situation: Mississippi river
Quantity: 1,500*f*
Title, Whence Derived: Spanish
Title Dated: 12 January 1789
Remarks: No evidence offered

Register's No.: 1,203
Present Claimant: **Samuel C. Young**
Original Claimant: **Alexander Pannill**
Situation: Bayou Sara
Quantity: 500*f*

Title, Whence Derived: Spanish
Title Dated: 27 February 1795
Remarks: No evidence offered

Register's No.: 1204
Present Claimant: **Samuel C. Young**
Original Claimant: **David Pannill**
Situation: Bayou Sara
Quantity: 500*f*
Title, Whence Derived: Spanish
Title Dated: 27 February 1795
Remarks: No evidence offered

Register's No.: 1232
Present Claimant: **Elijah Cushing**
Original Claimant: **Ithmer Andrews**
Situation: Big Black
Quantity: 100
Title, Whence Derived: British
Title Dated: 19 November 1778
Remarks: **Jeremiah Routh** says, "that Ithmer Andrews was about twenty-one years of age at the date of the warrant, and was, together with the inhabitants, driven out of that part of the country by the Indians."

Register's No.: 1245
Present Claimant: **R. King** and **P. King**
Original Claimant: **Justus King**
Situation: Homochitto river
Quantity: 100
Title, Whence Derived: British
Title Dated: --
Remarks: No warrant produced. **Caleb King** says, "that he was present, and carried the chain when the land was surveyed by one **Samuel Lewis**, a lawful surveyor, which was in the year 1776, and believes it was done under a warrant from the British Government of West Florida; that **James King** was living on the land with his family at the time the survey was run, and continued on it at least three years afterwards, and then was driven off by the Indians, and never resided on it again. After this it was included in a survey to **James Kirk**, under a grant of the Spanish Government to him, which prevented King's returning to it." The grant to Kirk has been confirmed by the commissioners."

Register's No.: 1273
Present Claimant: **Robert Starke**
Original Claimant: **Robert Starke**
Situation: Bayou Sara
Quantity: 2,000*f*

Title, Whence Derived: Spanish
Title Dated: 29 December 1791
Remarks: This land was regranted by the Spanish Government to **James Mather,** and a patent issued, which was confirmed by the commissioners. **Moses Johnson** says, "that, in 1791 or 1792, he cultivated the premises for the claimant with his negroes, and made two crops for the claimant, and, within the time he was cultivating the premises, the land was surveyed for the claimant by **William Atchison,** deputy surveyor under the Spanish Government. When the witness left the place it was in the possession of the claimant, and there was a crop of two or three hundred barrels of corn on the premises. The claimant was the head of a family at the date of the warrant." **Matthew McCulloch** says, "that, in the summer of the year 1794, he was present when Governor **[Manuel] Gayoso** and the claimant were conversing about the land in question, and heard the claimant say to Governor Gayoso that he would give up his then settlement on the land, if he, the Governor, would give him another piece of land which he had found; that the Governor turned round to Mr. Mather, who was present, and said, that, as he had been applying for land, this was fine tract, and he might have it; whereupon, the claimant said, 'Governor, observe, I do not mean to relinquish my settlement unless you give me the land which I found for it,' which was situated in the bayou Sara settlement. The Governor turned round to the claimant, and said to him he was a 'discontented old man,'" **Thomas Calvit** says, "that he believes **Robert Stark**, the claimant, was a resident in the Mississippi territory on the 27th October 1795."

Register's No.: 1276
Present Claimant: **T[homas] Tyler,** heirs of
Original Claimant: **Charles Bachelot**
Situation: Apple Island
Quantity: 2,065*f*
Title, Whence Derived: Spanish
Title Dated: Register's No.: December 1786
Remarks: This land was sold at public sale, and purchased by **Arthur Cobb**, 24 January 1789, who sold it to Thomas Tyler, 13 October, 1800. **George Fitzgerald** says, "that he knew Arthur Cobb to be a resident in the Mississippi territory before the yeear 1795, and believes he continued to be so until the year 1799, as he, the witness, was at his house, near the Spanish line of West Florida, at this time, where he was then living with his family." **William Kirkwood** says, "that, in the year 1788, and before then, the premises in question were inhabited and cultivated by one -- **Howard** for the use of the original grantee, Charles Bachelot; that, in that year, the whole island was overflowed, and Howard was obliged to move off; and that the owners annualy put stock on it, but no person inhabited it after the great flood till Tyler purchased it and afterwards Tyler built a cabin, and put a man in it to take care of his stock."

Register's No.: 1,278
Present Claimant: **Bennet Truly**
Original Claimant: **Richard Trivilian**
Situation: Bayou Pierre
Quantity: 336*f*
Title, Whence Derived: Spanish

Title Dated: --
Remarks: No warrant produced, but a certificate from **William Dunbar**, deputy surveyor, dated 10th March, 1795, stating that the land had been surveyed by virtue of a decree, or order of survey, from the Governor General.

Register's No.: 1279
Present Claimant: **Bennet Truly**
Original Claimant: **Edward Rose**
Situation: Bayou Pierre
Quantity: 400*f*
Title, Whence Derived: Spanish
Title Dated: 24 February 1795
Remarks: No evidence

Register's No.: 1290
Present Claimant: **Step[hen] Henderson**
Original Claimant: **William Vardiman**
Situation: Homochitto river
Quantity: 300*f*
Title, Whence Derived: Spanish
Title Dated: 28 September 1791
Remarks: No evidence

Register's No.: 1330
Present Claimant: **William Norris**
Original Claimant: **William Norris**
Situation: Homochitto river
Quantity: 200*f*
Title, Whence Derived: Spanish
Title Dated: 18 January 1793
Remarks: **John Searcy** says, "that the claimant was twenty-one years of age at the date of the warrant; that, in the fall of the year 1795, the claimant left the territory, and moved into the Opelousas country, and has remained there ever since; and there never was any improvement made on the premises till the year 1803, when **James Willis** cleared three or four acres, and planted it in corn, but the witness does not know whether on account of the claimant or not; neither does the witness know when the land was surveyd, or by what authority."

Register's No.: 1345
Present Claimant: **Nathaniel Tomlinson,** in right of his wife, **Elizabeth [Tomlinson]**
Original Claimant: **Elizabeth Baker**
Situation: Second cree,
Quantity: 800*f*
Title, Whence Derived: Spanish
Title Dated: 26 April 1790

Remarks: **Benjamin Newman** says, "that Elizabeth Baker was of age at the date of the warrant, and that neither of the claimants ever inhabited or cultivated the land." **Samuel Hutchins** says, "that, fifteen or sixteen years ago ('91 or '92) he was on the premises in question, at the house of **David Mitchell,** who told this witness that he was making an improvement on the land for Mrs. Baker, now the wife of this claimant; and that, some times afterwards, Mrs. Baker told the witness that Mitchell did improve the land for her. The witness also says, that, some short time afterwards, he applied in person to the surveyor for a certificate from him of the land now in question, being vacant, who told this witness that he could not give him one, as he had, some time prior to that, given one to Mrs. Baker for the premises."

Register's No.: 1352
Present Claimant: **Israel Leonard**
Original Claimant: **Abraham Knapp**
Situation: River Big Black
Quantity: 100
Title, Whence Derived: British
Title Dated: 19 November 1779
Remarks: No evidence

Register's No.: 1354
Present Claimant: **Caleb King**
Original Claimant: **Caleb King**
Situation: River Homochitto
Quantity: 300
Title, Whence Derived: British
Title Dated: Situation: August 1779
Remarks: **Nathan Swayze** says, "that the claimant was the head of a family at the date of the warrant, and inhabited and cultivated this land in 1776, and continued on it until he was driven off by the Indians, in or about the year 1780. The Spaniards afterwards took possession of the country, and granted a tract of land to **James Kirk,** who included the land in question in his survey; and that no person has resided on it or cultivated it since the claimant, King, left it." Kirk's patent has been confirmed by the commissioners.

(ASP 8:1:620)

Register's No.: 1358
Present Claimant: **Maurice Custard**
Original Claimant: **E. McKimm**
Situation: River Big Black
Quantity: 600*f*
Title, Whence Derived: Spanish
Title Dated: 24 February 1795
Remarks: **Jephtha Higdon** says, "that he knows the land in question; that it was surveyed in the year 1790, by **William Thomas** for **William Calvit,** who built a house thereon, and planted some peach stones. The witness does not know that any person lived in the house. The land is

situated in the Walnut bottom, on the road to the Walnut hills, adjoining lands of **Daniel Burnet** and **William Brocus.** The witness and **James Spain** carried the chain at the time of surveying."

Register's No.: 1360
Present Claimant: **Arthur Patterson**
Original Claimant: **Josiah Flowers**
Situation: Bayou Pierre
Quantity: 400
Title, Whence Derived: British
Title Dated: 19 November 1779
Remarks: No evidence

Register's No.: 1388
Present Claimant: **James Burnet**
Original Claimant: **James Burnet**
Situation: Big Black
Quantity: 1,180
Title, Whence Derived: Spanish
Title Dated: 23 March 1795
Remarks: No evidence

Register's No.: 1449
Present Claimant: **W[illiam] Scott,** heirs of
Original Claimant: **William Scott**
Situation: River Homochitto
Quantity: 400*f*
Title, Whence Derived: Spanish
Title Dated: 21 May 1787
Remarks: No evidence

Register's No.: 1471
Present Claimant: **Joshua Howard**
Original Claimant: **Joshua Howard**
Situation: Second creek
Quantity: 200
Title, Whence Derived: British
Title Dated: --
Remarks: No warrant produced, but a copy of the survey, from the field book of **Luke Collins**, formerly a deputy surveyor, which was proven to be the hand writing of said Luke Collins, dated the 28th of April 1800; also, a receipt for the surveying fees, dated 22 January 1777. **Henry Phipps** says, "that he carried one end of the chain when the land in question was surveyed. That the claimant, with his family, settled on the land previous to its being surveyed; that the witness lived with him at that time; and that the claimant continued to inhabit and cultivate it for three years after it was surveyed. The witness further says, that, in the latter part of the year 1779, the claimant left the premises in question, being dissatisfied with the Spanish Government.

Register's No.: 1501
Present Claimant: **John Smith**
Original Claimant: **Richard Winn**
Situation: Bayou Pierre
Quantity: 240*f*
Title, Whence Derived: Spanish
Title Dated: --
Remarks: No warrant produced, nor any other evidence offered in support of his claim, except a certificate of **William Dunbar**, dated 14th July 1790, stating that he had surveyed the land for Richard Winn, and given a plot thereof; but does not mention by what authority.

Register's No.: 1522
Present Claimant: **Joseph Vauchere'**
Original Claimant: **Joseph Vauchere'**
Situation: River Homochitto
Quantity: 600*f*
Title, Whence Derived: Spanish
Title Dated: --
Remarks: The only evidence produced is a certificate of **William Vousdan**, dated 28th October 1788, stating that he had surveyed the land for Joseph Vauchere', but names no authority for doing it.

Register's No.: 1524
Present Claimant: **David Ferguson**
Original Claimant: **James Dealy**
Situation: Bayou Sara
Quantity: 320*f*
Title, Whence Derived: Spanish
Title Dated: 17 January 1793
Remarks: No evidence

Register's No.: 1528
Present Claimant: **William Thomas**
Original Claimant: **William Thomas**
Situation: Bayou Pierre
Quantity: 600*f*
Title, Whence Derived: Spanish
Title Dated: -- February 1795
Remarks: **James Truly** says, "that the claimant was an actual settler in the Mississippi territory on the 27th October 1795."

Register's No.: 1531
Present Claimant: **William Thomas**
Original Claimant: **William Thomas**
Situation: Bayou Sara

Quantity: 280*f*
Title, Whence Derived: Spanish
Title Dated: 19 December 1793
Remarks: No evidence

Register's No.: 1537
Present Claimant: **George Cochran,** heirs of
Original Claimant: **Ralph Humphreys**
Situation: Bayou Pierre
Quantity: 169*f*
Title, Whence derived: Spanish
Title Dated: --
Remarks: No warrant produced. It is stated to be a part of a warrant for six hundred arpents, granted to Ralph Humphreys, dated 29th of January 1789. **William Smith** says, "that R. Humphreys was the head of a family at the date of the warrant, and cultivated the land in question in the year 1789 or 1790. There was then a cabin on it, and ten or twelve acres of cleared ground, which he purchased of **Reuben White**; the two following years it was cultivated by a certain **Benjamin Grubb**, for the use of the grantee. No further cultivation was made on it till sold to the claimant. **George W. Humphreys**, son and heir of the grantee, who sold to the claimant, was a resident in the Mississippi territory on the 27th October 1795."

Register's No.: 1568
Present Claimant: **Daniel Burnet**
Original Claimant: **Thomas Smith**
Situation: Bayou Pierre
Quantity: 210*f*
Title, Whence Derived: Spanish
Title Dated: 9 February 1790
Remarks: **Richard King** says, "that Thomas Smith was a resident in the Mississippi territory on the 27th of October, 1795."

Register's No.: 1574
Present Claimant: **D[aniel] Mygatt,** heirs of
Original Claimant: **Daniel Mygatt**
Situation: Bayou Pierre
Quantity: 100
Title, Whence Derived: British
Title Dated: 19 November 1779
Remarks: No evidence.

Register's No.: 1597
Present Claimant: **George Cochran**
Original Claimant: **George Cochran**
Situation: River Homochitto
Quantity: 300*f*

Title, Whence Derived: Spanish
Title Dated: 29 December 1791
Remarks: No evidence

Register's No.: 1619
Present Claimant: **Joseph Walker**
Original Claimant: **Joseph Walker**
Situation: Beaver creek
Quantity: 500*f*
Title, Whence Derived: Spanish
Title Dated: --
Remarks: The warrant to this claim was not produced. A certificate from **William Atchison,** dated in March 1795 stating that the claims, *severally*, were surveyed, in virtue of warrants from the Spanish Government, dated 30th of January 1795, were exhibited. William Atchison says "that there has been no cultivation on either of the tracts that he knows of; that Joseph Walker was of age at the date of the warrant, and was a resident in the Mississippi territory on the 27th October 1795."

Register's No.: 1620
Present Claimant: **John Walker**
Original Claimant: **John Walker**
Situation: Beaver creek
Quantity: 500*f*
Title, Whence Derived: Spanish
Title Dated: --
Remarks: See remarks at Register's No. 1619.

Register's No.: 1621
Present Claimant: **Peter Walker, Junior**
Original Claimant: **Peter Walker, Junior**
Situation: Beaver creek
Quantity: 500*f*
Title, Whence Derived: Spanish
Title Dated: --
Remarks: See remarks at Register's No. 1619.

(ASP 8:1:621)

Register's No.: 1641
Present Claimant: **Thomas Carter**
Original Claimant: **Thomas Carter**
Situation: Cole's creek
Quantity: --
Title, Whence Derived: British
Title Dated: --

Remarks: No warrant produced, and the quantity claimed not mentioned.

Register's No.: 1642
Present Claimant: **Henry Day**
Original Claimant: **Benjamin Day**
Situation: River Big Black
Quantity: 1,400
Title, Whence Derived: British
Title Dated: 19 November 1779* (*so stated)
Remarks: No evidence

Register's No.: 1643
Present Claimant: **Henry Day**
Original Claimant: **Henry Dwight**
Situation: River Big Black
Quantity: 1,100
Title, Whence Derived: British
Title Dated: 19 November 1778* (*so stated)
Remarks: No evidence

Register's No.: 1658
Present Claimant: **James Cole**
Original Claimant: **James Cole**
Situation: Lot No. 4, square No. 12, Natchez
Quantity: --
Title, Whence Derived: Spanish
Title Dated: 6 June 1795
Remarks: **Thomas Regar** says, "That the grantee was twenty-one years of age at the date of the warrant and, that some time early in the fall of the year 1795, the claimant had timber hauled to build a house, on the lot in question, and took the witness upon the lot to show him, and to get him assist in building the house; that, soon afterwards, the claimant was ordered to the Chickasaw bluffs, by the Spanish Government, and from thence he went to the States, and did not return until the year 1798." This lot was regranted by the Spanish Government and cnfirmed by the commissioners.

Register's No.: 1741
Present Claimant: **William Dunbar**
Original Claimant: **William Dunbar**
Situation: Thompson's creek
Quantity: 1,200
Title, Whence Derived: British
Title Dated: 16 September 1777
Remarks: No evidence.

Register's No.: 1742
Present Claimant: **David Roberts**
Original Claimant: **David Roberts**
Situation: River Big Black
Quantity: 240*f*
Title, Whence Derived: Spanish
Title Dated: 26 April 1790
Remarks: No evidence.

Register's No.: 1760
Present Claimant: **John Burnet, Junior**
Original Claimant: **John Burnet, Junior**
Situation: Bayou Pierre
Quantity: 130*f*
Title, Whence Derived: Spanish
Title Dated: 9 July 1782
Remarks: No evidence.

Register's No.: 1762
Present Claimant: -- **Neille** and -- **Beauvais**
Original Claimant: **John Cavamack?**
Situation: Bayou Sara
Quantity: 400*f*
Title, Whence Derived: Spanish
Title Dated: 27 February 1795
Remarks: No evidence.

Register's No.: 1775
Present Claimant: **S[ilas] Crane,** heirs of
Original Claimant: **Silas Crane**
Situation: River Homochitto
Quantity: 300
Title, Whence Derived: British
Title Dated: 19 November 1778
Remarks: **Richard King** says, "That he, the witness, understood that the land in question was surveyed in the year 1778 or 1779, by **Samuel Lewis**, then a deputy surveyor under the British Government; but that no settlement has been made on it by the claimants, or any person for them that he knows of."

Register's No.: 1780
Present Claimant: **Francis Brezina**
Original Claimant: **Francis Brezina**
Situation: River Homochitto
Quantity: 2,000*f*
Title, Whence Derived: Spanish

Title Dated: --
Remarks: No warrant produced, nor any evidence offered.

Register's No.: 1794
Present Claimant: **Frederick Mann**
Original Claimant: **Frederick Mann**
Situation: Bayou Sara
Quantity: 600*f*
Title, Whence Derived: Spanish
Title Dated: --
Remarks: No evidence of title produced, except a petition by the claimant to the Governor General, dated 31st January 1795, with a recommendation thereon for five hundred arpents by Governor **[Manuel] Gayoso.**

Register's No.: 1797
Present Claimant: **Ebenezer Rees**
Original Claimant: **James McGill**
Situation: Bayou Pierre
Quantity: 500*f*
Title, Whence Derived: Spanish
Title Dated: --
Remarks: No warrant produced.

Register's No.: 1799
Present Claimant: **Ebenezer Rees**
Original Claimant: **Ezina Baker**
Situation: Homochitto river
Quantity: 400*f*
Title, Whence Derived: Spanish
Title Dated: 24 February 1795
Remarks: No evidence

Register's No.: 1800
Present Claimant: **Silas L. Payne**
Original Claimant: **Joseph King**
Situation: Bayou Pierre
Quantity: 240*f*
Title, Whence Derived: Spanish
Title Dated: 26 April 1790
Remarks: No evidence

Register's No.: 1805
Present Claimant: **Daniel Finnan**
Original Claimant: **Daniel Finnan**
Situation: Bayou Pierre

Quantity: 240*f*
Title, Whence Derived: Spanish
Title Dated: 26 April 1790
Remarks: No evidence.

Register's No.: 1806
Present Claimant: **Jacob Stampley**
Original Claimant: **Jacob Stampley**
Situation: Homochitto river
Quantity: 200*f*
Title, Whence Derived: Spanish
Title Dated: 18 January 1793
Remarks: No evidence

Register's No.: 1808
Present Claimant: **Ebenezer Rees**
Original Claimant: **Jesse Lum**
Situation: Bayou Pierre
Quantity: 200*f*
Title, Whence Derived: Spanish
Title Dated: 18 January 1793
Remarks: No evidence

Register's No.: 1810
Present Claimant: **Ebenezer Rees**
Original Claimant: **Joseph Sticker**
Situation: Bayou Sara
Quantity: 400*f*
Title, Whence Derived: Spanish
Title Dated: 27 January 1790
Remarks: No evidence

Register's No.: 1807
Present Claimant: **Ebenezer Rees**
Original Claimant: **Robert Davis**
Situation: Thompson's creek
Quantity: 800*f*
Title, Whence Derived: Spanish
Title Dated: --
Remarks: No warrant produced, nor other evidence of title, except a petition of **Robert Davis** to the Governor General **[Manuel Gayoso],** dated 9th January 1795, and a recommendation thereon by Governor Gayoso

Register's No.: 1816
Present Claimant: **Ebenezer Rees**
Original Claimant: **Ebenezer Rees**
Situation: Bayou Sara
Quantity: 1,000*f*
Title, Whence Derived: Spanish
Title Dated: --
Remarks: No warrant produced, nor other evidence of title, except a petition from the claimant to the Governor General [**Manuel Gayoso**], dated 1st January 1795, and a recommendation thereon by Manuel Gayoso, Governor of Natchez, dated 2d January 1795.

Register's No.: 1849
Present Claimant: **Jeremiah Bryan**
Original Claimant: **Jeremiah Bryan**
Situation: Buffalo creek
Quantity: 800*f*
Title, Whence Derived: Spanish
Title Dated: Remarks: November 1788
Remarks: No evidence.

Register's No.: 1829
Present Claimant: **T[homas] Tyler,** heirs of
Original Claimant: **Thomas Tyler**
Situation: Bayou Pierre
Quantity: 1,000*f*
Title, Whence Derived: Spanish
Title Dated: --
Remarks: No warrant produced, nor other evidence of title, except a petition to the Governor General [**Manuel Gayoso**], dated the 7th of April 1795, with Governor Gayoso's recommendation thereon, and a certificate of **William Dunbar**, with a plot, dated 7th April 1795.

Register's No.: 1855
Present Claimant: **Bennet Truly**
Original Claimant: **Hugh Logan**
Situation: Bayou Pierre
Quantity: 240*f*
Title, Whence Derived: Spanish
Title Dated: Title Dated: April 1791
Remarks: No evidence.

Register's No.: 1856
Present Claimant: **Bennet Truly**
Original Claimant: **Bennet Truly**
Situation: Bayou Sara

Quantity: 200*f*
Title, Whence Derived: Spanish
Title Dated: Original Claimant: 3 January 1787
Remarks: No evidence.

Register's No.: 1857
Present Claimant: **William Ferguson,** heirs of
Original Claimant: **William Williams**
Situation: Cole's creek
Quantity: 500
Title, Whence Derived: British
Title Dated: 21 April 1779
Remarks: No evidence.

Register's No.: 1869
Present Claimant: **Peter B. Bruin**
Original Claimant: **Peter B. Bruin**
Situation: Bayou Pierre
Quantity: 500*f*
Title, Whence Derived: Spanish
Title Dated: 15 June 1795
Remarks: No evidence.

Register's No.: 1883
Present Claimant: **Robert Smith**
Original Claimant: **Robert Smith**
Situation: Bayou Pierre
Quantity: 200*f*
Title, Whence Derived: Spanish
Title Date: 18 January 1793
Remarks: No evidence.

Register's No.: 1885
Present Claimant: **Winthrop Sargent**
Original Claimant: **Maria Williams**
Situation: Lots No. 1 and 3, Square No. 5, Natchez
Quantity: --
Title, Whence Derived: Spanish
Title Dated: 30 September 1795
Remarks: No evidence.

Register's No.: 1895
Present Claimant: **Sarah Davis**
Original Claimant: **S. Coleby** & others
Situation: Bayou Pierre

Quantity: 400
Title, Whence Derived: British
Title Dated: 21 February 1778
Remarks: No evidence.

Register's No.: 1917
Present Claimant: **Thomas Fortner**
Original Claimant: **Thomas Fortner**
Situation: River Big Black
Quantity: 940*f*
Title, Whence Derived: Spanish
Title Dated: 26 April 1790
Remarks: **Vincent Fortner** says, "That the claimant was about eighteen years of age at the date of the warrant; and began to cultivate the premises in the year 1799, and has continued to so ever since, but has never lived on them, being a single man, until lately, but is now married and about to move on the premises; and there are about seven acres cleared, and a dwelling house and one out house.

(ASP 8:1:622)

Register's No.: 1925
Present Claimant: **Samuel Brooks**
Original Claimant: **William Silkrigs**
Situation: Mississippi River
Quantity: 200
Title, Whence Derived: British
Title Dated: --
Remarks: No warrant produced, but a certificate of a survey made the 21 August 1777; and a certificate of **William Vousdan**, formerly a deputy surveyor, dated in 1801. **Anthony Hutchins** says, "That the signature to the abovementioned certificate is the hand writing of William Vousdan, who, on the 21st of August, 1777, was a deputy surveyor for this district, under the British Government of West Florida; and that Silkrigs was twenty-one years of age, and upwards, at the date of the survey." **John Girault** says, "That William Silkrigs was an actual settler in the Mississippi territory on the 27th October 1795." William Silkrigs, sworn on the *voire dire*, says, "That he is in no instance interested in this claim at present; that he, the witness, in the year 1777, began to improve this land, and built him a house, and cleared and fenced in about three acres; and the next year lived as overseer to one of his neighbors, yet cultivated a crop on the same place, and gathered it in, and hauled it to the house of the person where he lived, and then went off and staid about two months, and returned to his land again, and the Americans took him as a prisoner, and carried him down the river in the year 1779, and remained with the Americans some time, and was afterwards re-taken by the British. By this time the Indians had plundered his place, and was thereby prevented from returning to it, and he continued down in the settled parts of the country, and continued there until lately, and obtained a Spanish grant in Adams County; that he, the witness, had a British warrant for the land in question; and under that warrant Mr. Vousdan surveyed the lands; that he, the witness, sent the warrant and survey to

Pensacola to get a patent, but they never returned; and that the premises were surveyed in the month of August 1777; the witness says he was twenty-one years of age in the year 1774."

Register's No.: 1926
Present Claimant: **P. M. McDermot**
Original Claimant: **P. M. McDermot**
Situation: Bayou Tunica
Quantity: 440*f*
Title, Whence Derived: Spanish
Title Dated: 18 January 1793
Remarks: **Narsworthy Huter** says, "That this land was first settled in the year 1796 by the claimant, when he built a small cabin and cleared half an acre, and cultivated it in corn, and nothing more has been done to the premises since that time, that the witness knows of. The witness does not know the age of the grantee or patentee, but, from his appearnace, thought he was not twenty-one years of age in 1793." **Peter Shilling** says, "That the claimant, when he first came to this country, which he thinks was in the year 1790, he came to the house of the witness to undertake to build a mill for him, and that he then appeared to be a man grown, and was acting for himself, and the witness thinks he was two or three-and-twenty years of age at that time." **Patrick Foley** says: "That the claimant was upwards of twenty-one years of age at the date of the warrant, and the witness believes he was a resident in the Mississippi territory on and before the 27th October 1795."

Register's No.: 1927
Present Claimant: **John Choate**
Original Claimant: **John Choate**
Situation: Second creek
Quantity: 100
Title, Whence Derived: British
Title Dated: --
Remarks: No warrants produced, nor any other evidence of title offered.

Register's No.: 1928
Present Claimant: **John Choate**
Original Claimant: **John Choate**
Situation: Second creek
Quantity: 100
Title, Whence Derived: British
Title Dated: --
Remarks: No warrant produced, nor any other evidence of title offered.

Register's No.: 1929
Present Claimant: **Sarah Choate**
Original Claimant: **Sarah Choate**
Situation: St. Catherine's creek
Quantity: 500*f*

Title, Whence Derived: Spanish
Title Dated: --
Remarks: No warrant produced, nor any other evidence of title offered.

Register's No.: 1959
Present Claimant: **Samuel Brooks**
Original Claimant: **William Hubbard**
Situation: Bayou Pierre
Quantity: 100
Title, Whence Derived: British
Title Dated: 4 August 1779
Remarks: **James Harman** says, "That the original claimant was upwards of twenty-one years of age at the date of the warrant, and had a wife and ten children in the year 1774." **William Silkrigs** says: "That Hubbard, at the time of his decease, gave him all his papers and rights; that he afterwards got the abovementioned warrant and other papers out of the Spanish office, where they had been lodged, and that he sold the warrant to the claimant, and is not now interested in the claim, either one way or the other. The reason why no settlement was made on the land was because the Spaniards shortly after took the country; it being a soldier's right, Hubbard dare not survey the land. Hubbard was an old, infirm, poor man, and his wife and children were never in this country.

(ASP 8:1:623)

Register's No.: 1968
Present Claimant: **R. S. Blackburn**
Original Claimant: **R. S. Blackburn**
Situation: Mississippi
Quantity: 3,000*f*
Title, Whence Derived: Spanish
Title Dated: --
Remarks: No warrant produced, nor any other evidence produced in support of this claim.

Register's No.: 1969
Present Claimant: **John Lewis**
Original Claimant: **John Lewis**
Situation: Mississippi river
Quantity: 2,000*f*
Title, Whence Derived: Spanish
Title Dated: --
Remarks: No warrant produced, nor any other evidence produced in support of this claim.

Register's No.: 1970
Present Claimant: **John Lewis**
Original Claimant: **John Lewis**
Situation: Mississippi river

Quantity: 2,000f
Title, Whence Derived: Spanish
Title Dated: --
Remarks: No warrant produced, nor any other evidence produced in support of this claim.

Register's No.: 1972
Present Claimant: **R. S. Blackburn**
Original Claimant: **R. S. Blackburn**
Situation: Mississippi river
Quantity: 3,000f
Title, Whence Derived: Spanish
Title Dated: --
Remarks: No warrant produced, nor any other evidence produced in support of this claim.

Register's No.: 1988
Present Claimant: **John Girault**
Original Claimant: **John St. Germain**
Situation: Mississippi river
Quantity: 1,000f
Title, Whence Derived: Spanish
Title Dated: 16 December 1785
Remarks: No evidence

Register's No.: 1989
Present Claimant: **John Girault**
Original Claimant: **Henry Bachelot**
Situation: Mississippi river
Quantity: 600f
Title, Whence Derived: Spanish
Title Dated: 22 March 1785
Remarks: No evidence.

Register's No.: 1990
Present Claimant: **John Girault**
Original Claimant: **Hugh Logan**
Situation: Cole's creek
Quantity: 240f
Title, Whence Derived: Spanish
Title Dated: Title Dated: April 1791
Remarks: No evidence.

Register's No.: 2008
Present Claimant: **James Frazier**
Original Claimant: **James Frazier**
Situation: Tombigbee river

Quantity: 1,600*f*
Title, Whence Derived: Spanish
Title Dated: --
Remarks: No warrant produced.

Register's No.: 2013
Present Claimant: **Sol[omon] H. Wisdom**
Original Claimant: **Sol[omon] H. Wisdom**
Situation: Lot No. 4, of sq[uare] No. 13, Natchez
Quantity: --
Title, Whence Derived: Spanish
Title Dated: 3 October 1795
Remarks: This lot was regranted by the Spanish Government, and a patent issued, which was confirmed by the commissioners, to **James Moor. John Girault** says, "that the claimant was a resident of the Mississippi territory on the 27th October 1795, and was the head of a family at the date of the warrant.

Register's No.: 2022
Present Claimant: **Christ[opher?; -ian?] Connelly**
Original Claimant: **Tomasina Lord**
Situation: Lot No. 1, of sq[uare] No. 19, Natchez
Quantity: --
Title, Whence Derived: Spanish
Title Dated: --
Remarks: This lot was regarnted, and a patent issued to **William Dunbar**, which has been confirmed by the commissioners.

Register's No.: 2028
Present Claimant: **Peter Walker,** heirs of
Original Claimant: **Peter Walker**
Situation: Buffalo creek
Quantity: 800*f*
Title, Whence Derived: Spanish
Title Dated: --
Remarks: No warrant produced. **William Atchison** says, "that he is well acquainted with the premises in question, and also **Elijah Bunch**, (of whom Walker purchased); that, about the year 1793 or 1794, Bunch obtained leave, either written or verbal, from the Spanish Governor **[Manuel] Gayoso**, to go and settle the land in question, and he did so; and the Governor desired the witness, who was a deputy surveyor, not to trouble him, and Bunch continued to inhabit and cultivate it until he contracted to sell it to the claimant, which was in 1797 or 1798. The witness surveyed it for Walker about the time the contract was made, and he understood that it had never been surveyed before, but that Walker purchased Bunch's improvement, and surveyed the land under a warrant to himself.

31

Register's No.: 2035
Present Claimant: **William Foster**
Original Claimant: **William Foster**
Situation: Petty creek
Quantity: 240*f*
Title, Whence Derived: Spanish
Title Dated: 26 May 1790
Remarks: No evidence.

Register's No.: 2036
Present Claimant: **Francis Irvine**
Original Claimant: **Francis Irvine**
Situation: Homochitto river
Quantity: 240*f*
Title, Whence Derived: Spanish
Title Dated: 26 April 1970
Remarks: No evidence

Register's No.: 2037
Present Claimant: **James Stoddard**
Original Claimant: **James Stoddard**
Situation: Homochitto river
Quantity: 400*f*
Title, Whence Derived: Spanish
Title Dated: 26 April 1790
Remarks: No evidence.

Register's No.: 2038
Present Claimant: **Isaac Lathrop**
Original Claimant: **Isaac Lathrop**
Situation: Homochitto river
Quantity: 240*f*
Title, Whence Derived: Spanish
Title Dated: 26 April 1790
Remarks: No evidence

Register's No.: 2039
Present Claimant: **Peter Martin**
Original Claimant: **Peter Martin**
Situation: Cole's creek
Quantity: 240*f*
Title, Whence Derived: Spanish
Title Dated: 26 April 1790
Remarks: No evidence

Register's No.: 2040
Present Claimant: **Jacob Stephen**
Original Claimant: **Jacob Stephen**
Situation: Cole's creek
Quantity: 240*f*
Title, Whence Derived: Spanish
Title Dated: 26 April 1790
Remarks: No evidence.

Register's No.: 2041
Present Claimant: **John Sinclair**
Original Claimant: **John Sinclair**
Situation: Cole's creek
Quantity: 240*f*
Title, Whence Derived: Spanish
Title Dated: 26 April 1790
Remarks: No evidence.

Register's No.: 2042
Present Claimant: **Henry Quirk**
Original Claimant: **Henry Quirk**
Situation: Bayou Pierre
Quantity: 240*f*
Title, Whence Derived: Spanish
Title Dated: 26 April 1790
Remarks: No evidence.

Register's No.: 2043
Present Claimant: **William Ivers**
Original Claimant: **William Ivers**
Situation: Bayou Pierre
Quantity: 240*f*
Title, Whence Derived: Spanish
Title Dated: 26 April 1790
Remarks: No evidence.

Register's No.: 2044
Present Claimant: **William Estell**
Original Claimant: **William Estell**
Situation: Bayou Pierre
Quantity: 240*f*
Title, Whence Derived: Spanish
Title Dated: 26 April 1790
Remarks: No evidence.

Register's No.: 2045
Present Claimant: **Lambert de Selle**
Original Claimant: **Lambert de Selle**
Situation: Homochitto river
Quantity: 300*f*
Title, Whence Derived: Spanish
Title Dated: 25 November 1789
Remarks: No evidence.

Register's No.: 2046
Present Claimant: **Patrick Quinn**
Original Claimant: **Patrick Quinn**
Situation: Bayou Pierre
Quantity: 240*f*
Title, Whence Derived: Spanish
Title Dated: 26 April 1790
Remarks: No evidence.

Register's No.: 2047
Present Claimant: **Ephraim Story**
Original Claimant: **Ephraim Story**
Situation: River Big Black
Quantity: 300*f*
Title, Whence Derived: Spanish
Title Dated: 18 December 1789
Remarks: No evidence.

Register's No.: 2048
Present Claimant: **Jacob Paul**
Original Claimant: **Jacob Paul**
Situation: Bayou Pierre
Quantity: 240*f*
Title, Whence Derived: Spanish
Title Dated: 25 November 1789
Remarks: No evidence.

Register's No.: 2049
Present Claimant: **Edmund Falson**
Original Claimant: **Edmund Falson**
Situation: Buffalo creek
Quantity: 300*f*
Title, Whence Derived: Spanish
Title Dated: 30 June 1789
Remarks: No evidence.

Register's No.: 2050
Present Claimant: **Samuel Porter**
Original Claimant: **Samuel Porter**
Situation: Cole's creek
Quantity: 240*f*
Title, Whence Derived: Spanish
Title Dated: 7 April 1791
Remarks: No evidence.

Register's No.: 2051
Present Claimant: **Adam Pickles**
Original Claimant: **Adam Pickles**
Situation: Cole's creek
Quantity: 400*f*
Title, Whence Derived: Spanish
Title Dated: 2 March 1793
Remarks: No evidence.

Register's No.: 2052
Present Claimant: **Hezek[iah] Harman**
Original Claimant: **Hezek[iah] Harman**
Situation: Bayou Pierre
Quantity: 300*f*
Title, Whence Derived: Spanish
Title Dated: 16 January 1789
Remarks: No evidence.

Register's No.: 2053
Present Claimant: **Gabriel Fuzelier**
Original Claimant: **Gabriel Fuzelier**
Situation: River Homochitto
Quantity: 400*f*
Title, Whence Derived: Spanish
Title Dated: 16 January 1789
Remarks: No evidence.

Register's No.: 2055
Present Claimant: **Samuel Young**
Original Claimant: **Samuel Young**
Situation: Willing's Bayou
Quantity: 240*f*
Title, Whence Derived: Spanish
Title Dated: 25 November 1789
Remarks: No evidence.

Register's No.: 2056
Present Claimant: **Peter Bissardon**
Original Claimant: **Peter Bissardon**
Situation: Lot in Natchez
Quantity: --
Title, Whence Derived: Spanish
Title Dated: 2 February 1787
Remarks: No evidence.

Register's No.: 2057
Present Claimant: **P. C. Pegroux**
Original Claimant: **P. C. Pegroux**
Situation: Homochitto river
Quantity: 1,600 f
Title, Whence Derived: Spanish
Title Dated: 14 June 1786
Remarks: No evidence.

(ASP: 8:1:624)

D.-- Continued.

Register's No.: 1367
Present Claimant: **Hyram Swayze,** heirs of
Original Claimant: **Hiram Swayze**
Situation: Near Natchez
Quantity: 164
Title, Whence Derived: Spanish
Title Dated: 18 January 1793
Remarks: This warrant was granted by Governor **[Manuel] Gayoso**, and not by the Governor General. **Richard King** says, "that the grantee was twenty-one years of age at the date of the warrant, and the land was granted him as a bounty for military service. The claimants resided in the Mississippi territory on the 27 October 1795. Hiram Swayze lived on or near the land in question from the year 1782 until he died, which was some time in the year 1794." **Prosper King** says, "that Hyram Swayze inhabited and cultivated the land in question at the time of his death, and his family continued to live on it, and cultivate for about two years afterwards." The land was regranted, and a patent issued, which has been confirmed by the commissioners.
Land Office, west of Pearl River, 1 October 1808. [Signed] Thomas H. Williams, Register

(ASP: 8:1:625)

Claims founded on Spanish Patents legallly and fully executed, but not confirmed by the Board of Commissioners, the claimants being non-residents on the 27th day of October 1795.

Register's No.: 56
Present Claimant: **Samuel Young**
Original Claimant: **Samuel Young**
Situation: Bayou Sara
Quantity: 480
Patent Date -- April 1799
Remarks: Regranted and confirmed by the commissioners.

Register's No.: 365
Present Claimant: **Charles Forget**
Original Claimant: **John Vidal**
Situation: Lot in the city of Natchez
Quantity: --
Patent Date: 12 March 1795
Remarks: --

Register's No.: 497
Present Claimant: **John Bisland**
Original Claimant: **James Jones** and **Evan Jones**
Situation: Fairchild's creek
Quantity: 500
Patent Date: 22 Jun 1791
Remarks: --

Register's No.: 615
Present Claimant: **George Cochran,** heirs of
Original Claimant: **John Perry**
Situation: Bayou Pierre
Quantity: 1,000
Patent Date: 20 October 1788
Remarks: --

Register's No.: 623
Present Claimant: **George Cochran,** heirs of
Original Claimant: **Peter Belly**
Situation: Mississippi river
Quantity: 630
Patent Date: Register's No.: June 1792
Remarks: --

Register's No.: 1045
Present Claimant: **William Brown**
Original Claimant: **William Brown**
Situation: Bayou Pierre
Quantity: 250
Patent Date: 1 April 1789
Remarks: --

Register's No.: 1055
Present Claimant: **Daniel Hickey**
Original Claimant: **Daniel Hickey**
Situation: Sandy creek
Quantity: 1,200
Patent Date: 10 March 1789
Remarks: --

Register's No.: 1205
Present Claimant: **Samuel C. Young**
Original Claimant: **John Pannill**
Situation: Bayou Sara
Quantity: 800
Patent Date: 20 June 1795
Remarks: --

Register's No.: 1206
Present Claimant: **Samuel C. Young**
Original Claimant: **Joseph Pannill**
Situation: Bayou Sara
Quantity: 1,000
Patent Date: 20 June 1795
Remarks: --

Register's No.: 1230
Present Claimant: **William Lintot**
Original Claimant: **Hubbard Rowell**
Situation: Bayou Sara
Quantity: 850
Patent Date: Patent Date: May 1791
Remarks: --

Register's No.: 1430
Present Claimant: **James Moore**
Original Claimant: **George Proffit**
Situation: Sandy creek
Quantity: 800

Patent Date: 15 March 1789
Remarks: --

Register's No.: 1545
Present Claimant: **William Conway**
Original Claimant: **William Conway**
Situation: Buffalo creek
Quantity: 800
Patent Date: -- June 1787
Remarks: --

Register's No.: 1735
Present Claimant: **Robert Dow**
Original Claimant: **Robert Dow**
Situation: Cole's creek
Quantity: 4,000
Patent Date: 16 May 1791
Remarks: --

Register's No.: 1764
Present Claimant: -- **Neille** and -- **Beauvais**
Original Claimant: **William Collins**
Situation: Feliciana creek
Quantity: 500
Patent Date: 10 April 1795
Remarks: --

Register's No.: 1939
Present Claimant: **James Kennedy**
Original Claimant: **Peter Miro**
Situation: Buffalo creek
Quantity: 1,600
Patent Date: 9 June 1787
Remarks: Regranted, and confirmed by the commissioners

Register's No.: 1951
Present Claimant: **James Kennedy**
Original Claimant: **James Kennedy**
Situation: Near Loftus cliffs
Quantity: 1,000
Patent Date: 4 December 1787
Remarks: --

Register's No.: 1966
Present Claimant: **Stephen Ploche'**
Original Claimant: **Stephen Ploche'**
Situation: Charles's creek
Quantity: 1,000
Patent Date: 3 March 1789
Remarks: --

Register's No.: 2003
Present Claimant: **George Pollock**
Original Claimant: **-- Fuzelier de la Clare**
Situation: River Homochitto
Quantity: 1,100
Patent Date: 8 August 1789
Remarks: --

Register's No.: 2010
Present Claimant: **Claudio Baugaud**
Original Claimant: **Claudio Baugaud**
Situation: Lake of the Cross
Quantity: 1,000
Patent Date: 6 March 1789
Remarks: --

Register's No.: 2014
Present Claimant: **Claudio Baugaud**
Original Claimant: **Claudio Baugaud**
Situation: Lake of the Cross
Quantity: 1,034
Patent Date: 30 August 1794
Remarks: --

Total Qauntity: 17,144

Land Office, west of Pearl River, 1 October 1808   [signed] **Thomas M. Williams,** Register

Andrews, Ithmer, 12
Atchison, William, deputy surveyor, 01
Atchison, William, 03
Atchison, William, 09
Atchison, William, 11
Atchison, William, 13
Atchison, William, 19
Atchison, William, 30
Bachelot, Charles, 13
Bachelot, Henry, 29
Baker, Elizabeth, 14
Baker, Elizabeth, 15
Baker, Ezina, 22
Barber, Philip, 07
Baugaud, Claudio, 39
Baugaud, Claudio, 39
Bay, Elihu Hall, 04
Bealk, Benjamin, 07
Beauvais, --, 21
Beauvais, --, 38
Belly, Peter, 36
Bisland, John, 36
Bissardon, Peter, 35
Blackburn, R. S., 28
Blackburn, R. S., 29
Boardman, Charles, heirs of, 03
Boardman, Charles, 03
Boardman, Charles, heirs of, 03
Boardman, Charles, 03
Boil, John, 03
Brashears, Ann, 10
Brezina, Francis, 21
Brocus, William, 16
Brooks, Samuel, 26
Brooks, Samuel, 28
Brown, William, 37
Bruin, Peter B., 25
Bryan, Jeremiah, 24
Bunch, Elijah, 30
Burnet, Daniel, 16
Burnet, Daniel, 18
Burnet, James, 16
Burnet, John, Junior, 21
Calvit, Anthony, 05
Calvit, Thomas, 13

Calvit, William, 15
Carney, Martin, 01
Carter, Nehemiah, 03
Carter, Thomas, 19
Cavamack, John, 21
Choate, John, 27
Choate, John, 27
Choate, Sarah, 27
Claiborne, Ferdinand L., 06
Clare, William, 08
Cloud, Adam, 08
Cloud, Adam, 08
Cobb, Arthur, 13
Cochran, George, 01
Cochran, George, 18
Cochran, George, heirs of, 01
Cochran, George, heirs of, 01
Cochran, George, heirs of, 18
Cochran, George, heirs of, 36
Cochran, George, heirs of, 36
Cogan, Patrick, 07
Cole, James, 20
Coleby, S., 25
Collins, John, 06
Collins, Luke, 16
Connelly, Christopher, 30
Connelly, Christian, 30
Conway, William, 38
Crane, Silas, 21
Crunkleton, James, 07
Crunkleton, James, 08
Crunkleton, John, 07
Cushing, Elijah, 12
Custard, Maurice, 15
Davis, Robert, 23
Davis, Sarah, 25
Day, Benjamin, 20
Day, Henry, 20
Day, Henry, 20
De Selle, Lambert, 33
De la Clare. See Fuzelier de la Clare
Dealy, James, 17
Devall, Richard, 11
Dow, Robert, 38
Dunbar, William, 03

Dunbar, Robert, 06
Dunbar, Robert, 07
Dunbar, William, 03
Dunbar, William, 08
Dunbar, William, 10
Dunbar, William, 14
Dunbar, William, 17
Dunbar, William, 20
Dunbar, William, 24
Dunbar, William, 30
Dwight, Henry, 20
Dyson, Joseph, 07
Ellis, John, Colonel, 06
Ellis, John, 11
Erwine, William, 11
Estell, William, 32
Falson, Edmund, 33
Ferguson, --, 06
Ferguson, David, 17
Ferguson, William, heirs of, 25
Finnan, Daniel, 22
Fitzgerald, George, 13
Flowers, Josiah, 16
Foley, Patrick, 27
Forget, Charles, 36
Forman, W. G. 11
Fortner, Thomas, 26
Fortner, Vincent, 26
Foster, William, 31
Foy, Benjamin, 10
Frazier, James, 29
Fuzelier de la Clare, --, 39
Fuzelier, Gabriel, 34
Gaillard, Isaac, 04
Gaskins, John, 03
Gayoso, Manuel, Governor, 01
Gayoso, Manuel, Governor, 04
Gayoso, Manuel, Governor, 05
Gayoso, Manuel, Governor, 13
Gayoso, Manuel, Governor, 22
Gayoso, Manuel, Governor, 23
Gayoso, Manuel, Governor, 24
Gayoso, Manuel, Governor, 24
Gayoso, Manuel, Governor, 30
Gayoso, Manuel, Governor, 35

Germain, John St. See St. Germain
Girault, John, Colonel, 04
Girault, John, 04
Girault, John, 08
Girault, John, 10
Girault, John, 26
Girault, John, 29
Girault, John, 29
Girault, John, 29
Girault, John, 30
Green, Henry, 06
Green, Thomas, Colonel, 06
Grubb, Benjamin, 18
Harman, Hezekiah, 34
Harman, James, 28
Harrison, Richard, 07
Henderson, John, 03
Henderson, Stephen, 14
Henderson, William, 03
Hickey, Daniel, 37
Higdon, Jephtha, 15
Holt, John, 11
Howard, Joshua, 05
Howard, --, 13
Howard, Joshua, 16
Hubbard, William, 28
Humphreys, George W., 18
Humphreys, Ralph, 18
Hunt, A., 11
Hunter, Narsworthy. See Narsworthy Huter
Hutchins, Anthony, 03
Hutchins, Anthony, 26
Hutchins, Samuel, 15
Huter, Narsworthy, 27
Irvine, Francis, 31
Ivers, William, 32
Johnson, Isaac, 09
Johnson, Isaac, 10
Johnson, Moses, 13
Jones, Evan, 36
Jones, Francis, 06
Jones, James, 36
Jones, Thomas, 07
Kennedy, James, 38
Kennedy, James, 38

King, Caleb, 02
King, Caleb, 12
King, Caleb, 15
King, James, 12
King, James, 12
King, Justus, 02
King, Justus, 02
King, Justus, 12
King, P., 02
King, P., 12
King, P., 12
King, Prosper, 35
King, R., 02
King, R., 12
King, Richard, 18
King, Richard, 21
King, Richard, 35
Kirk, James, 15
Kirkland, Zachariah, 07
Kirkwood, William, 13
Knapp, Abraham, 15
Lathrop, Isaac, 31
Leonard, Israel, 15
Lewis, John, 28
Lewis, John, 28
Lewis, Samuel, surveyor, 02
Lewis, Samuel, surveyor, 12
Lewis, Samuel, 21
Lintot, William, 37
Lloyd, Joseph W. A., 05
Lloyd, Joseph W. A., 05
Logan, Hugh, 24
Logan, Hugh, 29
Lord, Tomasina, 30
Lum, Jesse, 23
Mann, Frederick, 22
Martin, Peter, 31
Mather, James, 13
Matthews, George, 08
Matthews, George, 08
McCoy, John, 04
McCulloch, Matthew, 13
McDermot, P. M., 27
McGill, James, 22
McKay, John, 04

McKay, Alexander, 04
McKimm, E., 15
Miller, Robert, 11
Minor, Stephen, Major, 10
Miro, Peter, 38
Mitchell, David, 15
Moor, James, 30
Moore, James, 37
Morgan, Jemima, 10
Morgan, Jemima, 11
Mygatt, Daniel, 18
Neille, --, 21
Neille, --, 38
Newman, Benjamin, 15
Norris, William, 14
Paine, Silas L., 11
Pannill, Alexander, 11
Pannill, David, 12
Pannill, John, 37
Pannill, Joseph, 37
Patterson, Arthur, 16
Paul, Jacob, 33
Payne, Silas L., 22
Pegroux, P. C., 35
Percy, Thomas, 05
Perry, John, 36
Phipps, Henry, 16
Pickles, Adam, 34
Ploche', Stephen, 39
Pollock, George, 39
Porter, Samuel, 34
Proffit, George, 37
Quinn, Patrick, 33
Quirk, Henry, 32
Rapalje, Garret, heirs of, 04
Rapalje, Garret, 04
Rapalje, Garret, 05
Rapalje, Garret, Junior, 04
Rapalje, George, 04
Rapalje, Isaac, 04
Rapalje, Jacques, 04
Rees, Ebenezer, 22
Rees, Ebenezer, 22
Rees, Ebenez, 23
Rees, Ebenezer, 23

Rees, Ebenezer, 23
Rees, Ebenezer, 24
Regar, Thomas, 20
Roach, Henry, 01
Roberts, David, 21
Roberts, John, 06
Rose, Edward, 14
Routh, Jeremiah, 12
Rowell, Hubbard, 37
Sargent, Winthrop, 25
Schackler. John. See John Shackler
Scott, William, heirs of, 16
Scott, William, 16
Searcy, John, 14
Selle, De. See De Selle
Shackler, John, 04
Shackler, John, 05
Sharp, Joseph, 11
Shilling, Peter, 27
Silkrigs, William, 26
Silkrigs, William, 28
Sinclair, John, 32
Smith, John, 17
Smith, Robert, 25
Smith, Thomas, 18
Smith, William, 18
Spain, James, 16
St. Germain, John, 29
Staempfle. See Stampley
Stampley, Henry, 08
Stampley, Jacob, 23
Stark, Robert, 13
Starke, Robert, 12
Starnes, Moses, 09
Staybraker, John, 07
Stephen, Jacob, 32
Sticker, Joseph, 23
Stockett, Samuel, 09
Stoddard, James, 31
Story, Ephraim, 33
Surget, Catherine, 09
Surget, Charles, 10
Surget, Peter, 09
Surget, Peter, 09
Swayze, Nathan, 02

Swayze, Hiram, 35
Swayze, Hyram, heirs of, 35
Swayze, Nathan, 02
Swayze, Nathan, 15
Swayze, Samuel, 02
Swayze, Samuel, 02
Swayze, Stephen, 02
Symmons, James, 07
Thomas, William, 01
Thomas, William, 06
Thomas, William, 08
Thomas, William, 10
Thomas, William, 15
Thomas, William, 17
Thomas, William, 17
Tomlinson, Elizabeth, 14
Tomlinson, Nathaniel, 14
Trivilian, Richard, 13
Trudeau, Charles, 03
Truly, Bennet, 06
Truly, Bennet, 13
Truly, Bennet, 14
Truly, Bennet, 24
Truly, Bennet, 24
Truly, James, 07
Truly, James, 17
Tyler, Thomas, 13
Tyler, Thomas, heirs of, 24
Tyler, Thomas, 24
Vardiman, William, 05
Vardiman, William, 14
Vauchere, Joseph, 17
Vidal, John, 36
Vousdan, William, 10
Vousdan, William, 17
Vousdan, William, 26
Walker, Joseph, 19
Walker, John, 19
Walker, Peter, Junior, 19
Walker, Peter, heirs of, 30
Walker, Peter, 30
Watkins, --, 05
White, Reuben, 18
Wikoff, William, 11
Williams, Maria, 25

Williams, Thomas H., Register, 35
Williams, Thomas M., Register, 39
Williams, William, 25
Willis, James, 14
Winn, Richard, 17
Wisdom, Solomon H., 30
Wooley, --, 06
Young, Samuel C., 11
Young, Samuel C., 12
Young, Samuel, 34
Young, Samuel, 36
Young, Samuel C., 37
Young, Samuel C., 37

Selections from **The American State Papers**
Monograph Number 7

SPANISH AND BRITISH LAND GRANTS

IN MISSISSIPPI TERRITORY, 1750-1784

CLIFFORD NEAL SMITH

First printing, September 1996   rz

FOREWORD

The American State Papers are official public documents printed privately long before the Congressional Printing Office existed. The printing of public documents during the very early Congresses was done without any general provision of law as to what should be printed. Even as early as 1829 the clerk of the House of Representatives reported that, for the period 1793-1803 not a vestige of manuscript and only a scattered few printed copies were extant. A contributing factor was the destruction of the Capitol building in 1814 by fire.

In 1821 a bill was passed which authorized the publication of 750 copies of all the documents that could be found. The documents were published by two private companies: Gales and Seaton, and Duff Green. Of the two publications, Gales and Seaton is the larger. The Duff Green collection of documents are less comprehensive than the Gales and Seaton collection, and there are many differences in the pagination, particularly in later volumes.

Both publishers appear to have divided the original documents into general subject categories: Foreign Affairs, Indian Affairs, Finance, Commerce and Navigation, Military Affairs, Naval Affairs, Post Office Department, Public Land, and Claim. For genealogical and family history researchers, the last two categories--Public Land and Claims--are the most valuable, and it is from these two categories that this monograph *Selections from* **The American State Papers** will be made. The Public Land category, in eight volumes, covers the period 1789-1837; the Claims category, in one volume, covers the period 1790-1823.

In 1972 an attempt was made to index all names in the Public Land and Claims categories of the American State Papers; the index, although monumental, is, however, not complete. All researchers are urged to read pages i through xxvii of

Phillip McMullin, editor, *Grassroots of America: A Computerized Index to the American State Papers: Land Grants and Claims (1789-1837) with Other Aids to Research* (Salt Lake City, Utah: Gendex Corporation, 1972).

The present *Selections from the American State Papers* are the selections, by narrower subject matter, from the Gales and Seaton edition, made by this compiler for the use of genealogists and family historians because the original volumes are now very rare and, no doubt, inaccessible to most researchers.

(ASP 8:1:626)

A Report of claims east of Pearl river, founded on British or Spanish warrants, or orders of survey, not confirmed by former laws regulating the grants of land in the Mississippi territory, which have been regularly filed with the register of the Land Office for said district.

Date: Notice: 02 February 1804
Notice Number: 01
Present Claimant: **Alexander McCullagh**
Original Claimant: **Alexander McCullagh**
Quantity in Acres/Arpents: 200
Situation: Tombigbee river
Title Derived: British patent
Date of Patent/Warrant/Survey: 06 April 1178
Remarks: Rejected

Date: 08 February 1804
Notice Number: 02
Present Claimant: **Otto V.T. Barbaree**
Original Claimant: **Robert Farmer**
Quantity in Acres/Arpents: 1,000
Situation: Tombigbee river
Title Derived: British patent
Date of Patent/Warrant/Survey: 06 August 1778
Remarks: Rejected.

Date: 08 February 1804
Notice Number: 03
Present Claimant: **Otto V. T. Barbaree**
Original Claimant: **Robert Farmer**
Quantity in Acres/Arpents: 800
Situation: Tombigbee river
Title Derived: British patent
Date of Patent/Warrant/Survey: 06 August 1778
Remarks: Rejected.

Date: 23 February 1804
Notice Number: 07
Present Claimant: **William Vardeman**
Original Claimant: **John Lott, Junior**
Quantity in Acres/Arpents: 300
Situation: Tombigbee river
Title Derived: British patent
Date of Patent/Warrant/Survey: 16 February 1778
Remarks: Rejected

Date: 25 February 1804
Notice Number: 24
Present Claimant: **John McIntosh,** heirs of
Original Claimant: **John McIntosh**
Quantity in Acres/Arpents: 500
Situation: Tombigbee river
Title Derived: British patent
Date of Patent/Warrant/Survey: 12 September 1775
Remarks: Rejected.

Date: 20 March 1804
Notice Number: 53
Present Claimant: **Cornelius McCurtin**
Original Claimant: **Cornelius McCurtin**
Quantity in Acres/Arpents: 480
Situation: Tombigbee river
Title Derived: Spanish warrant of survey
Date of Patent/Warrant/Survey: 06 January 1794
Remarks: Rejected.

Date: 19 March 1804
Notice Number: 74
Present Claimant: **Samuel Mims**
Original Claimant: **John Turnbull**
Quantity in Acres/Arpents: 1,000
Situation: Tombigbee river
Title Derived: Spanish warrant of survey
Date of Patent/Warrant/Survey: 31 July 1787
Remarks: Rejected.

Date: 20 March 1804
Notice Number: 80
Present Claimant: **James Fraser**
Original Claimant: **James Fraser**
Quantity in Acres/Arpents: 1,600
Situation: Tombigbee river
Title Derived: Spanish warrant of survey
Date of Patent/Warrant/Survey: 31 July 1787
Remarks: Rejected.

Date: 20 March 1804
Notice Number: 84
Present Claimant: **Young Gains**
Original Claimant: **Young Gains**
Quantity in Acres/Arpents: 780

Situation: Tombigbee river
Title Derived: Spanish warrant of survey
Date of Patent/Warrant/Survey: 22 October 1787
Remarks: Rejected.

Date: 21 March 1804
Notice Number: 94
Present Claimant: **Anthony Epaho**
Original Claimant: **John Turnbull**
Quantity in Acres/Arpents: 500
Situation: Tombigbee river
Title Derived: Spanish warrant of survey
Date of Patent/Warrant/Survey: 31 July 1787
Remarks: Rejected.

Date: 19 March 1804
Notice Number: 102
Present Claimant: **Francisco Foutinella**
Original Claimant: **Francisco Foutinella**
Quantity in Acres/Arpents: 800
Situation: Tombigbee river
Title Derived: Spanish warrant of survey
Date of Patent/Warrant/Survey: 16 June 1795
Remarks: Rejected.

Date: 23 March 1804
Notice Number: 103
Present Claimant: **Peter Frouillet,** heirs of
Original Claimant: **Peter Frouillet**
Quantity in Acres/Arpents: 800
Situation: Tombigbee river
Title Derived: Spanish warrant of survey
Date of Patent/Warrant/Survey: 09 February 1788
Remarks: Rejected.

Date: 24 March 1804
Notice Number: 107
Present Claimant: **John Baker**
Original Claimant: **John Baker**
Quantity in Acres/Arpents: 1,600
Situation: Tombigbee river
Title Derived: Spanish permit
Date of Patent/Warrant/Survey: 09 January 1787
Remarks: Rejected.

Date: 24 March 1804
Notice Number: 114
Present Claimant: **Elihu Hall Bay**
Original Claimant: **William Fradgley**
Quantity in Acres/Arpents: 173
Situation: Tombigbee river
Title Derived: British patent
Date of Patent/Warrant/Survey: 12 March 1776
Remarks: Rejected.

Date: 24 March 1804
Notice Number: 115
Present Claimant: **Elihu Hall Bay**
Original Claimant: **William Fradgley**
Quantity in Acres/Arpents: 27
Situation: Tombigbee river
Title Derived: British patent
Date of Patent/Warrant/Survey: 13 March 1776
Remarks: Rejected.

Date: 24 March 1804
Notice Number: 116
Present Claimant: **Elihu Hall Bay**
Original Claimant: **John Sutherland**
Quantity in Acres/Arpents: 500
Situation: Tombigbee river
Title Derived: British patent
Date of Patent/Warrant/Survey: 22 October 1779
Remarks: Rejected.

Date: 12 March 1804
Notice Number: 117
Present Claimant: **Augustin Rochan,** heirs of
Original Claimant: **Augustine Rochan**
Quantity in Acres/Arpents: 225
Situation: Tombigbee river
Title Derived: British patent
Date of Patent/Warrant/Survey: 04 December 1798
Remarks: Rejected.

Date: 12 March 1804
Notice Number: 118
Present Claimant: **Augustin Rochan,** heirs of
Original Claimant: **Augustin Rochan**
Quantity in Acres/Arpents: 550

Situation: Tombigbee river
Title Derived: British patents
Date of Patent/Warrant/Survey: 16 June 1777
Remarks: Rejected.

Date: 26 March 1804
Notice Number: 119
Present Claimant: **Francis Coleman**
Original Claimant: **Charles Walker**
Quantity in Acres/Arpents: 500
Situation: Tombigbee river
Title Derived: British patent
Date of Patent/Warrant/Survey: 27 January 1777
Remarks: Rejected.

Date: 26 March 1804
Notice Number: 120
Present Claimant: **Francis Coleman**
Original Claimant: **Abraham Little**
Quantity in Acres/Arpents: 100
Situation: Tombigbee river
Title Derived: British patents
Date of Patent/Warrant/Survey: 16 February 1778
Remarks: Rejected.

Date: 16 March 1804
Notice Number: 121
Present Claimant: **James Hoggatt**
Original Claimant: **William Wall**
Quantity in Acres/Arpents: 250
Situation: Tombigbee river
Title Derived: British patent
Date of Patent/Warrant/Survey: 20 March 1778
Remarks: Rejected.

Date: 14 March 1804
Notice Number: 122
Present Claimant: **Joshua Howard**
Original Claimant: **Arthur Moore**
Quantity in Acres/Arpents: 324
Situation: Tombigbee river
Title Derived: British patent
Date of Patent/Warrant/Survey: --
Remarks: Rejected.

Date: 26 March 1804
Notice Number: 123
Present Claimant: **Robert Abrahams**
Original Claimant: **Robert Abrahams**
Quantity in Acres/Arpents: 500
Situation: Tombigbee river
Title Derived: British warrant of survey
Date of Patent/Warrant/Survey: 15 December 1778
Remarks: Rejected.

Date: 30 March 1804
Notice Number: 181
Present Claimant: **Seth Dean**
Original Claimant: **Charles Walker**
Quantity in Acres/Arpents: 2,000
Situation: Tombigbee river
Title Derived: British patent
Date of Patent/Warrant/Survey: 03 April 1770
Remarks: Rejected.

Date: 31 March 1804
Notice Number: 182
Present Claimant: **Seth Dean**
Original Claimant: **Francis Juzan**
Quantity in Acres/Arpents: 1,000
Situation: Mobile river
Title Derived: --
Date of Patent/Warrant/Survey: --
Remarks: Rejected.

Date: 29 March 1804
Notice Number: 183
Present Claimant: **Seth Dean**
Original Claimant: **John Dawson**
Quantity in Acres/Arpents: 150
Situation: Waters of Tombigbee river
Title Derived: British patent
Date of Patent/Warrant/Survey: --
Remarks: Rejected.

Date: 30 March 1804
Notice Number: 194
Present Claimant: **Benjamin King**
Original Claimant: **William Jackson**
Quantity in Acres/Arpents: 350

Situation: Tombigbee river
Title Derived: --
Date of Patent/Warrant/Survey: --
Remarks: Rejected.

(ASP 8:1:627)

Date: 19 March 1804
Notice Number: 04
Present Claimant: **Otto V. T. Barbaree**
Original Claimant: **Peter Deforge**
Quantity in Acres/Arpents: 520
Situation: Tensaw river
Title Derived: Lease and release
Date of Patent/Warrant/Survey: Date: November 1768
Remarks: Rejected

Date: 19 March 1804
Notice Number: 05
Present Claimant: **Otto V. T. Barbaree**
Original Claimant: **Francis Daran**
Quantity in Acres/Arpents: 542
Situation: Tensaw river
Title Derived: Mesne conveyance
Date of Patent/Warrant/Survey: 11 June 1764
Remarks: Rejected.

Date: 19 March 1804
Notice Number: 07
Present Claimant: **Samuel Mims**
Original Claimant: **Samuel Mims**
Quantity in Acres/Arpents: 982
Situation: Alabama river
Title Derived: Spanish warrant of survey
Date of Patent/Warrant/Survey: 27 February 1787
Remarks: Withdrawn by the claimant.

Date: 19 March 1804
Notice Number: 08
Present Claimant: **William Powell,** heirs of
Original Claimant: **William Powell**
Quantity in Acres/Arpents: 800
Situation: Tombigbee river
Title Derived: Spanish warrant of survey
Date of Patent/Warrant/Survey: 10 June 1795

Remarks: Rejected. It was not received by the Board, being on Indian land.

Date: 19 March 1804
Notice Number: 09
Present Claimant: **Gerald Byrne**
Original Claimant: **Peter Biverest**
Quantity in Acres/Arpents: --
Situation: Tensaw river
Title Derived: Bill of sale
Date of Patent/Warrant/Survey: 12 June 1792
Remarks: Not received by the Board, being within Spanish boundary.

Date: 20 March 1804
Notice Number: 13
Present Claimant: **John Morris**
Original Claimant: **John Morris**
Quantity in Acres/Arpents: 400
Situation: Tombigbee river
Title Derived: Spanish warrant of survey
Date of Patent/Warrant/Survey: 22 October 1787
Remarks: Not received by the Board, being on Indian land.

Date: 20 March 1804
Notice Number: 14
Present Claimant: **Hardy Perry**
Original Claimant: **Hardy Perry**
Quantity in Acres/Arpents: 800
Situation: Tombigbee river
Title Derived: Spanish warrant of survey
Date of Patent/Warrant/Survey: 09 February 1778
Remarks: Not received by the Board, being on Indian land.

Date: 21 March 1804
Notice Number: 15
Present Claimant: **Anthony Aspaho**
Original Claimant: **John Turnbull**
Quantity in Acres/Arpents: 800
Situation: Tombigbee river
Title Derived: Spanish warrant of survey
Date of Patent/Warrant/Survey: 14 January 1790
Remarks: Rejected.

Date: 20 March 1804
Notice Number: 18
Present Claimant: **Narciso Broutin**
Original Claimant: **Narciso Broutin**
Quantity in Acres/Arpents: 400
Situation: Tombigbee river
Title Derived: Spanish warrant of survey
Date of Patent/Warrant/Survey: 14 September 1787
Remarks: Withdrawn.

Date: 19 March 1804
Notice Number: 22
Present Claimant: **John Johnson**
Original Claimant: **John Johnson**
Quantity in Acres/Arpents: 800
Situation: Tombigbee river
Title Derived: Spanish warrant of survey
Date of Patent/Warrant/Survey: 10 June 1795
Remarks: Not received by the Board, being on Indian lands.

Date: 23 March 1804
Notice Number: 27
Present Claimant: **Pitiagad Jurzan**
Original Claimant: **Peter Jurzan**
Quantity in Acres/Arpents: 558
Situation: Mobile river
Title Derived: Spanish warrant of survey
Date of Patent/Warrant/Survey: --
Remarks: Withdrawn.

Date: 23 March 1804
Notice Number: 35
Present Claimant: **Thomas Malone**
Original Claimant: **Thomas Malone**
Quantity in Acres/Arpents: --
Situation: Tombigbee river
Title Derived: Spanish warrant of survey
Date of Patent/Warrant/Survey: --
Remarks: Not received by the Board, being on Indian lands.

Date: 31 March 1804
Notice Number: 56
Present Claimant: **Young Gains**
Original Claimant: **Young Gains**
Quantity in Acres/Arpents: 800

Situation: Tombigbee river
Title Derived: Spanish warrant of title
Date of Patent/Warrant/Survey: -- 1797
Remarks: Not received by the Board, being on Indian lands.

Date: 31 March 1804
Notice Number: 60
Present Claimant: **John Baker**
Original Claimant: **John Baker**
Quantity in Acres/Arpents: --
Situation: Tombigbee river
Title Derived: Spanish warrant of survey
Date of Patent/Warrant/Survey: 10 June 1795
Remarks: Not received by the Board, being on Indian lands.

Date: 31 March 1804
Notice Number: 67
Present Claimant: **Samuel Mims**
Original Claimant: **William Clark**
Quantity in Acres/Arpents: 350
Situation: Alabama river
Title Derived: British patent
Date of Patent/Warrant/Survey: 06 August 1778
Remarks: Rejected.

Date: 31 March 1804
Notice Number: 68
Present Claimant: **Peter Deforge,** heirs of
Original Claimant: **Peter Deforge**
Quantity in Acres/Arpents: 108
Situation: Waters of Tensaw river
Title Derived: British patent
Date of Patent/Warrant/Survey: 16 April 1779
Remarks: Rejected.

Date: 31 March 1804
Notice Number: 69
Present Claimant: **Peter Deforge,** heirs of
Original Claimant: **Peter Deforge**
Quantity in Acres/Arpents: 250
Situation: Tensaw river
Title Derived: British patent
Date of Patent/Warrant/Survey: 13 October 1779
Remarks: Not received by the Board, being within the Spanish boundary.

Date: 04 April 1804
Notice Number: 70
Present Claimant: **Theodore Gillard**
Original Claimant: **Alen Grant**
Quantity in Acres/Arpents: 100
Situation: Briar creek
Title Derived: British patent
Date of Patent/Warrant/Survey: 04 October 1779
Remarks: Rejected.

Date: 04 April 1804
Notice Number: 71
Present Claimant: **George Burdon**
Original Claimant: **George Burdon**
Quantity in Acres/Arpents: 260
Situation: Escambia river
Title Derived: British patent
Date of Patent/Warrant/Survey: 29 January 1790
Remarks: Not received by the Board, being within the Spanish boundary.

Date: 04 April 1804
Notice Number: 72
Present Claimant: **Theodore Gillard**
Original Claimant: **Joseph Lamb**
Quantity in Acres/Arpents: 200
Situation: Escambia river
Title Derived: British patent
Date of Patent/Warrant/Survey: 02 March 1779
Remarks: Not received by the Board, being within the Spanish boundary.

Date: 04 April 1804
Notice Number: 73
Present Claimant: **George Burdon**
Original Claimant: **George Burdon**
Quantity in Acres/Arpents: 800
Situation: Briar creek
Title Derived: British patent
Date of Patent/Warrant/Survey: 17 August 1779
Remarks: Rejected.

Date: 04 April 1804
Notice Number: 74
Present Claimant: **George Burdon**
Original Claimant: **George Burdon**
Quantity in Acres/Arpents: 200

Situation: Briar creek
Title Derived: British patent
Date of Patent/Warrant/Survey: 17 August 1779
Remarks: Rejected.

Date: 04 April 1804
Notice Number: 75
Present Claimant: **Theodore Gillard**
Original Claimant: **Francis Lewis**
Quantity in Acres/Arpents: 300
Situation: Escambia river
Title Derived: British patent
Date of Patent/Warrant/Survey: 16 June 1777
Remarks: Not received by the Board, being within the Spanish boundary.

Date: 04 April 1804
Notice Number: 76
Present Claimant: **Theodore Gillard**
Original Claimant: **Charles Ward**
Quantity in Acres/Arpents: 500
Situation: Escambia river
Title Derived: British patent
Date of Patent/Warrant/Survey: 02 March 1779
Remarks: Not received by the Board, being within the Spanish boundary.

Date: 04 April 1804
Notice Number: 77
Present Claimant: **Theodore Gillard**
Original Claimant: **Charles Ward**
Quantity in Acres/Arpents: 500
Situation: Escambia river
Title Derived: British patent
Date of Patent/Warrant/Survey: -- March 1779
Remarks: Not received by the Board, being within the Spanish boundary.

Date: 11 June 1804
Notice Number: 83
Present Claimant: **Joseph Stiggins**
Original Claimant: **Joseph Stiggins**
Quantity in Acres/Arpents: 800
Situation: Tensaw lake
Title Derived: Spanish warrant of survey
Date of Patent/Warrant/Survey: 09 February 1788
Remarks: Rejected.

Date: 11 June 1804
Notice Number: 89
Present Claimant: **Abijah Hunt**
Original Claimant: **Augustin Rochan**
Quantity in Acres/Arpents: 1,000
Situation: Mobile river
Title Derived: Deed of conveyance
Date of Patent/Warrant/Survey: 16 December 1801
Remarks: Rejected.

Date: 30 April 1804
Notice Number: 90
Present Claimant: **Alexander McCullagh,** heirs of
Original Claimant: **Thomas Underwood**
Quantity in Acres/Arpents: 500
Situation: Alabama river
Title Derived: Deed of conveyance
Date of Patent/Warrant/Survey: 01 January 1779
Remarks: Rejected.

[Signed] **N. Perkins**, Register of the Land Office, east of Pearl River, Mississippi Territory.

(ASP 8:1:628)

[This page contains only a list of documents, registers, etc., forwarded from the General Land Office.]

(ASP 8:1:629)

Commissioners' Certificates: When entered: 14 August 1805
Commissioners' Certificates: Number: 04
Commissioners' Certificates: Date: 07 August 1805
Commissioners' Certificate: Recorded:Vol.Page: volume 01, page 66
Claim: To whom granted: The lawful heirs of **Thomas Bassett**, deceased, on application of Thomas Bassett, administrator of **Nathaniel Bassett**
Original Grantee: **Thomas Bassett,** deceased
Acreage: 750
Situation: West margin of Tombigbee
Title: Whence derived: West margin of Tombigbee
Title: Date of Patent: British
Title: Date of Patent: Destroyed in the fire at New Orleans in 1794.

Commissioners' Certificates: When entered: 14 August 1805
Commissioners' Certificates: Number: 03
Commissioners' Certificates: Date: 07 August 1805
Commissioners' Certificate: Recorded:Vol.Page: volume 01, page 68
Claim: To whom granted: Heirs of **Thomas Bassett,** deceased
Original Grantee: **Thomas Bassett,** deceased
Acreage: 1,050
Situation: West margin of Tombigbee
Title: Whence derived: British
Title: Date of Patent: Destroyed as above

Commissioners' Certificates: When entered: 03 September 185
Commissioners' Certificates: Number: 05
Commissioners' Certificates: Date: 07 August 1805
Commissioners' Certificate: Recorded:Vol.Page: volume 01, page 126
Claim: To whom granted: Heirs of **Maria Josepia Narbone,** deceased
Original Grantee: --
Acreage: 80
Situation: Both sides of west channel of Mobile
Title: Whence Derived: French
Title: Date of Patent: Sale & uninterrupted possession since.

Commissioners' Certificates: When entered: 03 September 1805
Commissioners' Certificates: Number: 02
Commissioners' Certificates: Date: 07 August 1805
Commissioners' Certificate: Recorded:Vol.Page: volume 01, page 128
Claim: To whom granted: Heirs of **Augustine Rochon,** deceased
Original Grantee: **Augustine Rochon,** deceased
Acreage: 550
Situation: West bank of Tombigbee
Title: Whence Derived: British
Title: Date of Patent: 16 June 1777

Commissioners' Certificates: When entered: 03 September 1805
Commissioners' Certificates: Number: 01
Commissioners' Certificates: Date: 07 August 1805
Commissioners' Certificate: Recorded:Vol.Page: volume 01, page 129
Claim: To whom granted: Heirs of **Augustine Rochon**, deceased
Original Grantee: **Augustine Rochon**, deceased
Acreage: 225
Situation: West bank of Tombigbee
Title: Whence Derived: British
Title: Date of Patent: 04 December 1779.

Commissioners' Certificates: When entered: 14 September 1805
Commissioners' Certificates: Number: 06
Commissioners' Certificates: Date: 29 August 1805
Commissioners' Certificate: Recorded:Vol.Page: volume 01, page 157
Claim: To whom granted: **Richard Carpenter, Caleb Carpenter,** and **Joseph Carpenter,** or their heirs or devisees
Original Grantee: **Richard Carpenter, Caleb Carpenter,** and **Joseph Carpenter**
Acreage: 1,000
Situation: East margin of the Alabama
Title: Whence Derived: British
Title: Date of Patent: 22 July 1769.

(ASP 8:1:630)

Commissioners' Certificates: When entered: 08 August 1805
Commissioners' Certificates: Number: 35
Commissioners certificates: Date: 07 August 1805
Commissioners' certificates: Recorded: volume 01, page 02
Claim: To whom granted: **Benjamin Harrison**
Original grantee or claimant: **Jacob Miller**
Acreage: 640
Situation: West side of Tombigbee
Whence derived: Occupancy
Date of order of survey or settlement: 1797.

Commissioners' Certificates: When entered: 08 August 1805
Commissioners' Certificates: Number: 29
Commissioners certificates: Date: 07 August 1805
Commissioners' certificates: Recorded: volume 01, page 04
Claim: To whom granted: **Wiley Barker**
Original grantee or claimant: **Daniel Barker**
Acreage: 640*
Situation: West side of Tombigbee
Whence derived: Occupancy
Date of order of survey or settlement: 1797
*If the lines include so much.

Commissioners' Certificates: When entered: 08 August 1805
Commissioners' Certificates: Number: 11
Commissioners certificates: Date: 07 August 1805
Commissioners' certificates: Recorded: volume 01, page 06
Claim: To whom granted: **James Denley**
Original grantee or claimant: **Daniel Ward**
Acreage: 1,000

Situation: West margin of Tombigbee
Whence derived: Spanish
Date of order of survey or settlement: 22 October 1787.

Commissioners' Certificates: When entered: 08 August 1805
Commissioners' Certificates: Number 14
Commissioners certificates: Date: 07 August 1805
Commissioners' certificates: Recorded: volume 01, page 09
Claim: To whom granted: **James Denley**
Original grantee or claimant: **Solomon Johnson**
Acreage: 280
Situation: West side of Tombigbee
Whence derived: Spanish
Date of order of survey or settlement: 10 June 1795

Commissioners' Certificates: When entered: 08 August 1805
Commissioners' Certificates: Number: 38
Commissioners certificates: Date: 07 August 1805
Commissioners' certificates: Recorded: volume 01, page 10
Claim: To whom granted: **Ephraim Barker**
Original grantee or claimant: **Ephraim Barker**
Acreage: 640
Situation: West margin of Tombigbee
Whence derived: Occupancy
Date of order of survey or settlement: 1797.

Commissioners' Certificates: When entered: 08 August 1805
Commissioners' Certificates: Number: 13
Commissioners certificates: Date: 07 August 1805
Commissioners' certificates: Recorded: volume 01, page 11
Claim: To whom granted: **James Denley**
Original grantee or claimant: **James Denley**
Acreage: 400
Situation: West margin of Tombigbee
Whence derived: Spanish
Date of order of survey or settlement: 22 October 1787.

Commissioners' Certificates: When entered: 08 August 1805
Commissioners' Certificates: Number: 54
Commissioners certificates: Date: 01 August 1805
Commissioners' certificates: Recorded: volume 01, page 13
Claim: To whom granted: **Adam Hollinger**
Original grantee or claimant: **Adam Hollinger**
Acreage: 1,000
Situation: East margin of Tombigbee

Whence derived: Spanish
Date of order of survey or settlement: 30 January 1795.

Commissioners' Certificates: When entered: 08 August 1805
Commissioners' Certificates: Number: 43
Commissioners certificates: Date: 07 August 1805
Commissioners' certificates: Recorded: volume 01, page 16
Claim: To whom granted: **Richard Hawkins**
Original grantee or claimant: **Richard Hawkins**
Acreage: 640
Situation: West side of Mobile river
Whence derived: Occupancy
Date of order of survey or settlement: 1797.

Commissioners' Certificates: When entered: 08 August 1805
Commissioners' Certificates: Number: 52
Commissioners certificates: Date: 01 August 1805
Commissioners' certificates: Recorded: volume 01, page 17
Claim: To whom granted: **Joseph Bates**
Original grantee or claimant: **Joseph Bates**
Acreage: 1,000*
Situation: East margin of Tombigbee
Whence derived: Spanish
Date of order of survey or settlement: 18 August 1795.
*If included in the lines.

Commissioners' Certificates: When entered: 08 Agustu 1805
Commissioners' Certificates: Number: 53
Commissioners certificates: Date: 01 August 1805
Commissioners' certificates: Recorded: volume 01, page 23
Claim: To whom granted: **Natt Christmas**
Original grantee or claimant: **Michael Hartly**
Acreage: 640
Situation: Fork of Tombigbee & Alabama
Whence derived: Occupancy
Date of order of survey or settlement: 1797.

Commissioners' Certificates: When entered: 08 August 1805
Commissioners' Certificates: Number: 44
Commissioners certificates: Date: 07 August 1805
Commissioners' certificates: Recorded: volume 01, page 25
Claim: To whom granted: **Young Gaines**
Original grantee or claimant: **Dominique Olive**
Acreage: 800
Situation: West margin of Tombigbee

Whence derived: Spanish
Date of order of survey or settlement: 15 March 1788.

Commissioners' Certificates: When entered: 09 August 1805
Commissioners' certificate: Number: 06
Commissioners certificates: Date: 07 August 1805
Commissioners' certificates: Recorded: volume 01, page 26
Claim: To whom granted: Heirs of **James McGrew**
Original grantee or claimant: **James McGrew**
Acreage: 400
Situation: West margin of Tombigbee
Whence derived: Spanish
Date of order of survey or settlement: 09 February 1788

Commissioners' Certificates: When entered: 10 August 1805
Commissioners' certificate: Number: 42
Commissioners certificates: Date: 07 August 1805
Commissioners' certificates: Recorded: volume 01, page 29
Claim: To whom granted: Heirs of **William Burke**
Original grantee or claimant: **Thomas Jones**
Acreage: 640*
Situation: West margin of Tombigbee
Whence derived: Occupancy
Date of order of survey or settlement: 1797.
*If the lines include so much.

Commissioners' Certificates: When entered: 10 August 1805
Commissioners' certificate: Number: 58
Commissioners certificates: Date: 01 August 1805
Commissioners' certificates: Recorded: volume 01, page 31
Claim: To whom granted: **John Weekley**
Original grantee or claimant: **James Farr**
Acreage: 639
Situation: East margin of Tensaw lake
Whence derived: Occupancy
Date of order of survey or settlement: 1797.

Commissioners' Certificates: When entered: 10 August 1805
Commissioners' certificate: Number: 55
Commissioners certificates: Date: 01 August 1805
Commissioners' certificates: Recorded: volume 01, page 32
Claim: To whom granted: **Benjamin Hooven**
Original grantee or claimant: **Benjamin Hooven**
Acreage: 566+
Situation: East margin of Alabama

Whence derived: Occupancy
Date of order of survey or settlement: 1797.
Commissioners' Certificates: When entered: 10 August 1805
Commissioners' certificate: Number: 56
Commissioners certificates: Date: 01 August 1805
Commissioners' certificates: Recorded: volume 01, page 34
Claim: To whom granted: **George Weekley**
Original grantee or claimant: **George Weekley**
Acreage: 640
Situation: East margin of Stedham's lake
Whence derived: Occupancy
Date of order of survey or settlement: 1797.

Commissioners' Certificates: When entered: 10 August 1805
Commissioners' certificate: Number: 57
Commissioners certificates: Date: 01 August 1805
Commissioners' certificates: Recorded: volume 01, page 35
Claim: To whom granted: **George Weekley**
Original grantee or claimant: **Michael Skipper**
Acreage: The quantity included in the lines
Situation: West margin of Alabama
Whence derived: Spanish
Date of order of survey or settlement: 09 February 1788.

Commissioners' Certificates: When entered: 12 August 1805
Commissioners' certificate: Number: 63
Commissioners certificates: Date: 01 August 1805
Commissioners' certificates: Recorded: volume 01, page 43
Claim: To whom granted: **Joseph Stiggins**
Original grantee or claimant: **John Johnson**
Acreage: 800
Situation: east margin of Tensaw lake
Whence derived: Spanish
Date of order of survey or settlement: 09 February 1788

Commissioners' Certificates: When entered: 12 August 1805
Commissioners' certificate: Number: 60
Commissioners certificates: Date: 01 August 1805
Commissioners' certificates: Recorded: volume 01, page 44
Claim: To whom granted: **Joseph Thompson**
Original grantee or claimant: **Joseph Thompson**
Acreage: 640
Situation: East margin of Hollow creek
Whence derived: Occupancy
Date of order of survey or settlement: 1797.

Commissioners' Certificates: When entered: 12 August 1805
Commissioners' certificate: Number: 20
Commissioners certificates: Date: 01 August 1805
Commissioners' certificates: Recorded: volume 01, page 46
Claim: To whom granted: **Moses Stedham**
Original grantee or claimant: **Moses Stedham**
Acreage: 628
Situation: Margin of Stedham's lake
Whence derived: Occupancy
Date of order of survey or settlement: 1797

Commissioners' Certificates: When entered: 12 August 1805
Commissioners' certificate: Number: 59
Commissioners certificates: Date: 01 August 1805
Commissioners' certificates: Recorded: volume 01, page 47
Claim: To whom granted: **Samuel Mims**
Original grantee or claimant: **Samuel Mims**
Acreage: 640
Situation: South margin of the Cut-off
Whence derived: Occupancy
Date of order of survey or settlement: 1797

Commissioners' Certificates: When entered: 12 August 1805
Commissioners' certificate: Number: 61
Commissioners certificates: Date: 01 August 1805
Commissioners' certificates: Recorded: volume 01, page 49
Claim: To whom granted: **Joseph Thompson**
Original grantee or claimant: **Adam Holinger**
Acreage: 730
Situation: West margin of the Alabama
Whence derived: Spanish
Date of order of survey or settlement: 22 October 1787.

Commissioners' Certificates: When entered: 12 August 1805
Commissioners' certificate: Number: 67
Commissioners certificates: Date: 01 August 1805
Commissioners' certificates: Recorded: volume 01, page 51
Claim: To whom granted: **Simeon Wilks**
Original grantee or claimant: **James Proctor**
Acreage: 640
Situation: East side of Mobile river
Whence derived: Occupancy
Date of order of survey or settlement: 1797.

Commissioners' Certificates: When entered: 12 August 1805
Commissioners' certificate: Number: 66
Commissioners certificates: Date: 01 August 1805
Commissioners' certificates: Recorded: volume 01, page 52
Claim: To whom granted: **Reuben Dyer**
Original grantee or claimant: **Reuben Dyer**
Acreage: 640
Situation: Margin of the Tensaw river
Whence derived: Occupancy
Date of order of survey or settlement: 1797.

Commissioners' Certificates: When entered: 12 August 1805
Commissioners' certificate: Number: 64
Commissioners certificates: Date: 01 August 1805
Commissioners' certificates: Recorded: volume 01, page 53
Claim: To whom granted: **Samuel Frend**
Original grantee or claimant: **Samuel Frend**
Acreage: 640
Situation: East side of Mobile river
Whence derived: Occupancy
Date of order of survey or settlement: 1797.

Commissioners' Certificates: When entered: 12 August 1805
Commissioners' certificate: Number: 65
Commissioners certificates: Date: 01 August 1805
Commissioners' certificates: Recorded: volume 01, page 55
Claim: To whom granted: **John Randon**
Original grantee or claimant: **John Randon**
Acreage: 301
Situation: West margin of Alabama
Whence derived: Occupancy
Date of order of survey or settlement: 1797.

Commissioners' Certificates: When entered: 12 August 1805
Commissioners' certificate: Number: 62
Commissioners certificates: Date: 01 August 1805
Commissioners' certificates: Recorded: volume 01, page 58
Claim: To whom granted: **Joseph Stiggins**
Original grantee or claimant: **Joseph Stiggins**
Acreage: 635
Situation: Margin of Tensaw lake
Whence derived: Occupancy
Date of order of survey or settlement: 1797.

Commissioners' Certificates: When entered: 14 August 1805
Commissioners' certificate: Number: 04
Commissioners certificates: Date: 07 August 1805
Commissioners' certificates: Recorded: volume 01, page 60
Claim: To whom granted: **Nicholas Perkins**
Original grantee or claimant: **Thomas Wheat**
Acreage: 306
Situation: West margin of Tombigbee
Whence derived: Spanish
Date of order of survey or settlement: 22 October 1787.

Commissioners' Certificates: When entered: 14 August 1805
Commissioners' certificate: Number: 25
Commissioners certificates: Date: 07 August 1805
Commissioners' certificates: Recorded: volume 01, page 61
Claim: To whom granted: **Howel Dupree**
Original grantee or claimant: **William Hillis**
Acreage: 613
Situation: West margin of Mobile river
Whence derived: Occupancy
Date of order of survey or settlement: 1797.

Commissioners' Certificates: When entered: 14 August 1805
Commissioners' certificate: Number: 03
Commissioners certificates: Date: 07 August 1805
Commissioners' certificates: Recorded: volume 01, page 63
Claim: To whom granted: **Nicholas Perkins**
Original grantee or claimant: **Daniel Johnson**
Acreage: 200
Situation: West margin of Tombigbee
Whence derived: Spanish
Date of order of survey or settlement: 22 October 1787.

Commissioners' Certificates: When entered: 14 August 1805
Commissioners' certificate: Number: 39
Commissioners certificates: Date: 07 August 1805
Commissioners' certificates: Recorded: volume 01, page 64
Claim: To whom granted: Heirs of **Godfrey Helverson**
Original grantee or claimant: **Godfrey Helverson**
Acreage: 640
Situation: West bank of Mobile river
Whence derived: Occupancy
Date of order of survey or settlement: 1797.

Commissioners' Certificates: When entered: 14 August 1805
Commissioners' certificate: Number: 65
Commissioners certificates: Date: 07 August 1805
Commissioners' certificates: Recorded: volume 01, page 65
Claim: To whom granted: **Thomas Bates**
Original grantee or claimant: **Thomas Bates**
Acreage: 628
Situation: West margin of Tombigbee
Whence derived: Occupancy
Date of order of survey or settlement: 1797.

Commissioners' Certificates: When entered: 14 August 1805
Commissioners' certificate: Number: 05
Commissioners certificates: Date: 07 August 1805
Commissioners' certificates: Recorded: volume 01, page 69
Claim: To whom granted: Heirs of **Owen Sullivan**, deceased, on application of **J. Hinson**, administrator of **Owen Sullivan,** deceased
Original grantee or claimant: **Owen Sullivan,** deceased
Acreage: 400
Situation: West margin of Tombigbee
Whence derived: Spanish
Date of order of survey or settlement: 10 June 1795.

Commissioners' Certificates: When entered: 15 August 1805
Commissioners' certificate: Number: 18
Commissioners certificates: Date: 07 August 1805
Commissioners' certificates: Recorded: volume 01, page 72
Claim: To whom granted: Heirs of **James Copelen,** deceased
Original grantee or claimant: **James Copelen**, deceased
Acreage: 640
Situation: West margin of Three River lake
Whence derived: Occupancy
Date of order of survey or settlement: 1797.

Commissioners' Certificates: When entered: 16 August 1805
Commissioners' certificate: Number: 40
Commissioners certificates: Date: 07 August 1805
Commissioners' certificates: Recorded: volume 01, page 74
Claim: To whom granted: **George Brewer, Junior**
Original grantee or claimant: **George Brewer, Junior**
Acreage: 629
Situation: West margin of Tombigbee river
Whence derived: Occupancy
Date of order of survey or settlement: 1797.

Commissioners' Certificates: When entered: 16 August 1805
Commissioners' certificate: Number: 19
Commissioners certificates: Date: 07 August 1805
Commissioners' certificates: Recorded: volume 01, page 75
Claim: To whom granted: **James Griffin**
Original grantee or claimant: **James Griffin**
Acreage: 640
Situation: West side of Tombigbee
Whence derived: Occupancy
Date of order of survey or settlement: 1797.

Commissioners' Certificates: When entered: 16 August 1805
Commissioners' certificate: Number: 47
Commissioners certificates: Date: 07 August 1805
Commissioners' certificates: Recorded: volume 01, page 77
Claim: To whom granted: **George Brewer, Junior**
Original grantee or claimant: **Valentine Dubroca**
Acreage: 800
Situation: West margin of Tombigbee
Whence derived: Spanish
Date of order of survey or settlement: 22 October 1787.

Commissioners' Certificates: When entered: 16 August 1805
Commissioners' certificate: Number: 02
Commissioners certificates: Date: 07 August 1805
Commissioners' certificates: Recorded: volume 01, page 78
Claim: To whom granted: Heirs of **William Powell,** deceased
Original grantee or claimant: **William Powell,** deceased
Acreage: 400
Situation: West margin of Tombigbee
Whence derived: Spanish
Date of order of survey or settlement: 10 June 1795.

Commissioners' Certificates: When entered: 16 August 1805
Commissioners' certificate: Number: 27
Commissioners certificates: Date: 07 August 1805
Commissioners' certificates: Recorded: volume 01, page 80
Claim: To whom granted: **George Brewer, Junior**
Original grantee or claimant: **James Watkins**
Acreage: 620
Situation: West side of Tombigbee
Whence derived: Occupancy
Date of order of survey or settlement: 1797.

Commissioners' Certificates: When entered: 17 August 1805
Commissioners' certificate: Number: 23
Commissioners certificates: Date: 07 August 1805
Commissioners' certificates: Recorded: volume 01, page 82
Claim: To whom granted: **Thomas Carson**
Original grantee or claimant: **John Jacob Abner**
Acreage: 640
Situation: West margin of Tombigbee
Whence derived: Occupancy
Date of order of survey or settlement: 1797.

Commissioners' Certificates: When entered: 17 Aug 1805
Commissioners' certificate: Number: 72
Commissioners certificates: Date: 01 August 1805
Commissioners' certificates: Recorded: 85
Claim: To whom granted: **John Mills**
Original grantee or claimant: **John Mills**
Acreage: Whatever may be included in the lines, not exceeding 640 acres
Situation: West margin of Alabama
Whence derived: Occupancy
Date of order of survey or settlement: 1797.

Commissioners' Certificates: When entered: 17 August 1805
Commissioners' certificate: Number: 75
Commissioners certificates: Date: 01 August 1805
Commissioners' certificates: Recorded: volume 01, page 86
Claim: To whom granted: **Abraham Walker**
Original grantee or claimant: **Abraham Walker**
Acreage: 630
Situation: East margin of Hollow creek
Whence derived: Occupancy
Date of order of survey or settlement: 1797.

Commissioners' Certificates: When entered: 17 August 1805
Commissioners' certificate: Number: 70
Commissioners certificates: Date: 01 August 1805
Commissioners' certificates: Recorded: volume 01, page 88
Claim: To whom granted: **Francis Killingworth**
Original grantee or claimant: **William Mills**
Acreage: 640
Situation: East margin of Pine log creek
Whence derived: Occupancy
Date of order of survey or settlement: 1797.

Commissioners' Certificates: When entered: 17 August 1805
Commissioners' certificate: Number: 73
Commissioners certificates: Date: 01 August 1805
Commissioners' certificates: Recorded: volume 01, page 89
Claim: To whom granted: **Lemuel Henry**
Original grantee or claimant: **John Linder, Senior**
Acreage: 491
Situation: Tensaw lake and Alabama
Whence derived: Spanish
Date of order of survey or settlement: 03 June 1788.

Commissioners' Certificates: When entered: 17 August 1805
Commissioners' certificate: Number: 71
Commissioners certificates: Date: 01 August 1805
Commissioners' certificates: Recorded: volume 01, page 91
Claim: To whom granted: Heirs of **John Linder, Junior**
Original grantee or claimant: **John Linder, Junior**
Acreage: 800, if included in the lines
Situation: Tensaw lake and Alabama
Whence derived: Spanish
Date of order of survey or settlement: 03 June 1788.

Commissioners' Certificates: When entered: 21 August 1805
Commissioners' certificate: Number: 51
Commissioners certificates: Date: 07 August 1805
Commissioners' certificates: Recorded: volume 01, page 94
Claim: To whom granted: **Simon Andry**
Original grantee or claimant: **Simon Andry**
Acreage: 48
Situation: East bank of west channel Mobile
Whence derived: Spanish
Date of order of survey or settlement: 02 February 1793.

Commissioners' Certificates: When entered: 21 August 1805
Commissioners' certificate: Number: 49
Commissioners certificates: Date: 07 August 1805
Commissioners' certificates: Recorded: volume 01, page 96
Claim: To whom granted: **Joseph Chastang**
Original grantee or claimant: **Joseph Chastang**
Acreage: 640
Situation: West bank of the Mobile river
Whence derived: Occupancy
Date of order of survey or settlement: 1797.

Commissioners' Certificates: When entered: 21 August 1805
Commissioners' certificate: Number: 06
Commissioners certificates: Date: 07 August 1805
Commissioners' certificates: Recorded: volume 01, page 97
Claim: To whom granted: **Doctor John Chastang**
Original grantee or claimant: **Doctor John Chastang**
Acreage: 480
Situation: West margin of Tombigbee
Whence derived: Spanish
Date of order of survey or settlement: 30 January 1795.

Commissioners' Certificates: When entered: 21 August 1805
Commissioners' certificate: Number: 07
Commissioners certificates: Date: 07 August 1805
Commissioners' certificates: Recorded: volume 01, page 98
Claim: To whom granted: **Doctor John Chastang**
Original grantee or claimant: **John Talley**
Acreage: 480
Situation: West margin of Tombigbee
Whence derived: Spanish
Date of order of survey or settlement: 27 November 1787.

Commissioners' Certificates: When entered: 21 August 1805
Commissioners' certificate: Number: 46
Commissioners certificates: Date: 07 August 1805
Commissioners' certificates: Recorded: volume 01, page 99
Claim: To whom granted: **John Chastang**
Original grantee or claimant: **John Chastang**
Acreage: 1,938
Situation: West side of west channel Mobile
Whence derived: Spanish
Date of order of survey or settlement: 18 January 1795.

Commissioners' Certificates: When entered: 21 August 1805
Commissioners' certificate: Number: 09
Commissioners certificates: Date: 07 August 1805
Commissioners' certificates: Recorded: volume 01, page 102
Claim: To whom granted: **Simon Andry**
Original grantee or claimant: **Simon Andry**
Acreage: 480
Situation: West margin of Mobile river
Whence derived: Spanish
Date of order of survey or settlement: 14 May 1787.

Commissioners' Certificates: When entered: 23 August 1805
Commissioners' certificate: Number: 74
Commissioners certificates: Date: 19 August 1805
Commissioners' certificates: Recorded: volume 01, page 103
Claim: To whom granted: **William McDaniel**
Original grantee or claimant: **George Phillips**
Acreage: 632
Situation: Major's creek, east side of Mobile
Whence derived: Occupancy
Date of order of survey or settlement: 1797.

Commissioners' Certificates: When entered: 23 August 1805
Commissioners' certificate: Number: 32
Commissioners certificates: Date: 17 August 1805
Commissioners' certificates: Recorded: volume 01, page 104
Claim: To whom granted: **Isaac Ryan**
Original grantee or claimant: **Isaac Ryan**
Acreage: 640
Situation: Bassett's creek
Whence derived: Occupancy
Date of order of survey or settlement: 1797.

Commissioners' Certificates: When entered: 24 August 1805
Commissioners' certificate: Number: 80
Commissioners certificates: Date: 01 August 1805
Commissioners' certificates: Recorded: volume 01, page 105
Claim: To whom granted: **Josiah Fletcher**
Original grantee or claimant: **Josiah Fletcher**
Acreage: Whatever the lines may include, not exceeding 640 acres.
Situation: West margin of Alabama
Whence derived: Occupancy
Date of order of survey or settlement: 1797.

Commissioners' Certificates: When entered: 29 August 1805
Commissioners' certificate: Number: 10
Commissioners certificates: Date: 07 August 1805
Commissioners' certificates: Recorded: voume 01, page 109
Claim: To whom granted: **John Baptiste Trennier**
Original grantee or claimant: **John Baptiste Trennier**
Acreage: 327
Situation: West margin of Mobile river
Whence derived: Spanish
Date of order of survey or settlement: 01 September 1787.

Commissioners' Certificates: When entered: 29 August 1805
Commissioners' certificate: Number: 50
Commissioners certificates: Date: 07 August 1805
Commissioners' certificates: Recorded: volume 01, page 111
Claim: To whom granted: **John Baptiste Trennier**
Original grantee or claimant: **John Baptiste Trennier**
Acreage: 1,000
Situation: East bank of west channel Mobile
Whence derived: Spanish
Date of order of survey or settlement: 14 October 1790.

Commissioners' Certificates: When entered: 29 August 1805
Commissioners' certificate: Number: 68
Commissioners certificates: Date: 07 August 1805
Commissioners' certificates: Recorded: voume 01, page 112
Claim: To whom granted: **Thomas Malone**
Original grantee or claimant: **John Arnot**
Acreage: 480
Situation: West margin of Tombigbee
Whence derived: Spanish
Date of order of survey or settlement: 02 July 1787.

Commissioners' Certificates: When entered: 29 August 1805
Commissioners' certificate: Number: 87
Commissioners certificates: Date: 01 August 1805
Commissioners' certificates: Recorded: volume 01, page 114
Claim: To whom granted: Heirs of **Dominique De Olive**
Original grantee or claimant: **Dominique De Olive**
Acreage: 1,200
Situation: East margin of Mobile river
Whence derived: Spanish
Date of order of survey or settlement: 06 December 1794.

Commissioners' Certificates: When entered: 02 September 1805
Commissioners' certificate: Number: 83
Commissioners certificates: Date: 01 August 1805
Commissioners' certificates: Recorded: volume 01, page 120
Claim: To whom granted: **Richard Coleman**
Original grantee or claimant: **Richard Coleman**
Acreage: 634
Situation: East margin of Tensaw lake
Whence derived: Occupancy
Date of order of survey or settlement: 1797.

Commissioners' Certificates: When entered: 03 September 1805
Commissioners' certificate: Number: 78
Commissioners certificates: Date: 04 August 1805
Commissioners' certificates: Recorded: volume 01, page 123
Claim: To whom granted: **Joseph Campbell**
Original grantee or claimant: **Augustine Rochon**
Acreage: 400
Situation: East margin of Mobile
Whence derived: Spanish
Date of order of survey or settlement: 09 March 1794.

Commissioners' Certificates: When entered: 03 September 1805
Commissioners' certificate: Number: 79
Commissioners certificates: Date: 04 August 1805
Commissioners' certificates: Recorded: volume 01, page 124
Claim: To whom granted: **Joseph Campbell**
Original grantee or claimant: **Louisa Rochon**
Acreage: 400
Situation: East margin of Mobile
Whence derived: Spanish
Date of order of survey or settlement: 09 March 1794.

Commissioners' Certificates: When entered: 04 September 1805
Commissioners' certificate: Number: 81
Commissioners certificates: Date: 01 August 1805
Commissioners' certificates: Recorded: volume 01, page 134.
Claim: To whom granted: **Frances Steel**
Original grantee or claimant: **Frances Steel**
Acreage: 640
Situation: Tensaw lake
Whence derived: Occupancy
Date of order of survey or settlement: 1797.

Commissioners' Certificates: When entered: 05 September 1805
Commissioners' certificate: Number: 88
Commissioners certificates: Date: 05 September 1805
Commissioners' certificates: Recorded: volume 01, page 137
Claim: To whom granted: **Narciso Broutin**
Original grantee or claimant: **Narciso Broutin**
Acreage: 800
Situation: East margine of Mobile river
Whence derived: Spanish
Date of order of survey or settlement: 10 January 1794.

Commissioners' Certificates: When entered: 07 September 1805
Commissioners' certificate: Number: 82
Commissioners certificates: Date: 01 August 1805
Commissioners' certificates: Recorded: volume 01, page 138
Claim: To whom granted: The heirs of **Michael Milton**
Original grantee or claimant: **Michael Milton**
Acreage: 611
Situation: South margin of Tensaw lake
Whence derived: Occupancy
Date of order of survey or settlement: 1797.

Commissioners' Certificates: When entered: 09 September 1805
Commissioners' certificate: Number: 76
Commissioners certificates: Date: 22 August 1805
Commissioners' certificates: Recorded: volume 01, page 139
Claim: To whom granted: **William Buford**
Original grantee or claimant: **Conrad Selhoof**
Acreage: 800
Situation: East margin of Tensaw river
Whence derived: Spanish
Date of order of survey or settlement: 09 February 1788.

Commissioners' Certificates: When entered: 09 September 1805
Commissioners' certificate: Number: 85
Commissioners certificates: Date: 01 August 1805
Commissioners' certificates: Recorded: volume 01, page 142
Claim: To whom granted: **William Pierce** and **John Pierce**
Original grantee or claimant: **Jeremiah Phillips**
Acreage: 640
Situation: West margin of Alabama
Whence derived: Occupancy
Date of order of survey or settlement: 1797.

Commissioners' Certificates: When entered: 14 September 1805
Commissioners' certificate: Number: 48
Commissioners certificates: Date: 07 August 1805
Commissioners' certificates: Recorded: volume 01, page 143
Claim: To whom granted: **John Brewer**
Original grantee or claimant: **Charfles Arbon Demoy**
Acreage: 800
Situation: West margin of Tombigbee
Whence derived: Spanish
Date of order of survey or settlement: 22 October 1787.

Commissioners' Certificates: When entered: 14 September 1805
Commissioners' certificate: Number: 28
Commissioners certificates: Date: 07 August 1805
Commissioners' certificates: Recorded: volume 01, page 144
Claim: To whom granted: **John Brewer**
Original grantee or claimant: **John Brewer**
Acreage: 640
Situation: West side of Tombigbee
Whence derived: Occupancy
Date of order of survey or settlement: 1797.

Commissioners' Certificates: When entered: 14 September 1805
Commissioners' certificate: Number: 21
Commissioners certificates: Date: 07 August 1805
Commissioners' certificates: Recorded: volume 01, page 145
Claim: To whom granted: **Daniel Johnson**
Original grantee or claimant: **William Burke**
Acreage: 320
Situation: Margin of Three River lake
Whence derived: Occupancy
Date of order of survey or settlement: 1797.

Commissioners' Certificates: When entered: 14 September 1805
Commissioners' certificate: Number: 86
Commissioners certificates: Date: 01 August 1805
Commissioners' certificates: Recorded: volume 01, page 147
Claim: To whom granted: **William Webber**
Original grantee or claimant: **William Webber**
Acreage: 640
Situation: East side of the Mobile
Whence derived: Occupancy
Date of order of survey or settlement: 1797.

Commissioners' Certificates: When entered: 14 September 1805
Commissioners' certificate: Number: 12
Commissioners certificates: Date: 07 August 1805
Commissioners' certificates: Recorded: volume 01, page 148
Claim: To whom granted: **Francis Boykin**
Original grantee or claimant: **Adam Hollinger**
Acreage: 800
Situation: West margin of Tombigbee
Whence derived: Spanish
Date of order of survey or settlement: 10 June 1795.

Commissioners' Certificates: When entered: 14 September 1805
Commissioners' certificate: Number: 33
Commissioners certificates: Date: 07 August 1805
Commissioners' certificates: Recorded: volume 01, page 150
Claim: To whom granted: Heirs of **Matthew Bilbo,** deceased
Original grantee or claimant: **Matthew Bilbo,** deceased
Acreage: 401
Situation: Island in the Tombigbee
Whence derived: Occupancy
Date of order of survey or settlement: 1797.

Commissioners' Certificates: When entered: 14 September 1805
Commissioners' certificate: Number: 17
Commissioners certificates: Date: 07 August 1805
Commissioners' certificates: Recorded: volume 01, page 150
Claim: To whom granted: **Hardy Wooton**
Original grantee or claimant: **William Hunt**
Acreage: 615
Situation: West side of Tombigbee
Whence derived: Occupancy
Date of order of survey or settlement: 1797.

Commissioners' Certificates: When entered: 14 March 1805
Commissioners' certificate: Number: 30
Commissioners certificates: Date: 07 August 1805
Commissioners' certificates: Recorded: volume 01, page 154
Claim: To whom granted: **Richard Lee**
Original grantee or claimant: **Jordan Morgan**
Acreage: 640
Situation: West side of Tombigbee
Whence derived: Occupancy
Date of order of survey or settlement: 1797.

Commissioners' Certificates: When entered: 14 September 1805
Commissioners' certificate: Number: 37
Commissioners certificates: Date: 07 August 1805
Commissioners' certificates: Recorded: volume 01, page 156
Claim: To whom granted: **Richard Barrow**
Original grantee or claimant: **Richard Barrow**
Acreage: 640
Situation: West bank of Mobile river
Whence derived: Occupancy
Date of order of survey or settlement: 1797.

34

Commissioners' Certificates: When entered: 16 September 1805
Commissioners' certificate: Number: 84
Commissioners certificates: Date: 01 August 1805
Commissioners' certificates: Recorded: volume 01, page 158
Claim: To whom granted: **James Mills**
Original grantee or claimant: **John Linder, Senior**
Acreage: 299
Situation: East side of the Mobile
Whence derived: Spanish
Date of order of survey or settlement: 03 June 1788.

Commissioners' Certificates: When entered: 18 September 1805
Commissioners' certificate: Number: 34
Commissioners certificates: Date: 23 August 1805
Commissioners' certificates: Recorded: volume 01, page 160
Claim: To whom granted: **James Scott**
Original grantee or claimant: **Gabriel Barrows**
Acreage: 375
Situation: West side of Tombigbee
Whence derived: Occupancy
Date of order of survey or settlement: 1797.

Commissioners' Certificates: When entered: 19 September 1805
Commissioners' certificate: Number: 36
Commissioners certificates: Date: 22 August 1805
Commissioners' certificates: Recorded: volume 01, page 163
Claim: To whom granted: **Nathan Blackwell**
Original grantee or claimant: **Nathan Blackwell**
Acreage: 640
Situation: West margin of Tombigbee
Whence derived: Occupancy
Date of order of survey or settlement: 1797.

Commissioners' Certificates: When entered: 26 September 1805
Commissioners' certificate: Number: 26
Commissioners certificates: Date: 07 August 1805
Commissioners' certificates: Recorded: volume 01, page 171
Claim: To whom granted: **Ann Lawrence**
Original grantee or claimant: **Ann Lawrence**
Acreage: 445
Situation: West margin of Tombigbee
Whence derived: Occupancy
Date of order of survey or settlement: 1797.

Commissioners' Certificates: When entered: 28 September 1805
Commissioners' certificate: Number: 01
Commissioners certificates: Date: 07 August 1805
Commissioners' certificates: Recorded: volume 01, page 175
Claim: To whom granted: **John F. McGrew** and **Clarke McGrew**
Original grantee or claimant: **Julian De Castro**
Acreage: 400
Situation: West margin of Tombigbee
Whence derived: Spanish
Date of order of survey or settlement: 10 June 1795.

Commissioners' Certificates: When entered: 28 September 1805
Commissioners' certificate: Number: 15
Commissioners certificates: Date: 01 August 1805
Commissioners' certificates: Recorded: volume 01, page 179
Claim: To whom granted: **James Cockaram**
Original grantee or claimant: **Samuel Lyons**
Acreage: 640
Situation: Waters of Rice creek
Whence derived: Occupancy
Date of order of survey or settlement: 1797.

Commissioners' Certificates: When entered: 30 September 1805
Commissioners' certificate: Number: 27
Commissioners certificates: Date: 22 August 1805
Commissioners' certificates: Recorded: volume 01, page 180
Claim: To whom granted: **James Callier**
Original grantee or claimant: **Joseph Campbell**
Acreage: 640
Situation: East margin of Mobile river
Whence derived: Occupancy
Date of order of survey or settlement: 1797.

Commissioners' Certificates: When entered: 30 September 1805
Commissioners' certificate: Number: 24
Commissioners certificates: Date: 07 August 1805
Commissioners' certificates: Recorded: volume 01, page 181
Claim: To whom granted: **James Callier**
Original grantee or claimant: **Jesse Bryant** and **Henry Snelgrove**
Acreage: 573
Situation: West margin of Tombigbee
Whence derived: Occupancy
Date of order of survey or settlement: 1797.

Commissioners' Certificates: When entered: 24 September 1805
Commissioners' certificate: Number: 31
Commissioners certificates: Date: 07 August 1805
Commissioners' certificates: Recorded: volume 01, page 207
Claim: To whom granted: **Anna Munger**
Original grantee or claimant: **Anna Munger**
Acreage: 504
Situation: West m,argin of Tombigbee
Whence derived: Occupancy
Date of order of survey or settlement: 1797.

Commissioners' Certificates: When entered: 24 September 1805
Commissioners' certificate: Number: 22
Commissioners certificates: Date: 24 August 1805
Commissioners' certificates: Recorded: volume 01, page 208
Claim: To whom granted: **Hiram Munger**
Original grantee or claimant: **Hiram Munger**
Acreage: 640
Situation: West side of Tombigbee
Whence derived: Occupancy
Date of order of survey or settlement: 1797.

Commissioners' Certificates: When entered: 24 September 1805
Commissioners' certificate: Number: 41
Commissioners certificates: Date: 07 August 1805
Commissioners' certificates: Recorded: volume 01, page 210
Claim: To whom granted: **Sampson Munger**
Original grantee or claimant: **Sampson Munger**
Acreage: 634
Situation: West side of Tombigbee
Whence derived: Occupancy
Date of order of survey or settlement: 1797.

INDEX

Abner, John Jacob, 25
Abrahams, Robert, 6
Andry, Simon, 26
Andry, Simon, 27
Arbon. See Demoy
Arnot, John, 29
Aspaho, Anthony, 8
Aspaho. See also Epaho
Baker, John, 3
Baker, John, 10
Barbaree, Otto V. T., 1
Barbaree, Otto V.T., 1
Barbaree, Otto V. T., 7
Barbaree, Otto V. T., 7
Barker, Wiley, 15
Barker, Daniel, 15
Barker, Ephraim, 16
Barrow, Richard, 33
Barrows, Gabriel, 34
Bassett, Nathaniel, 13
Bassett, Thomas, deceased, heirs of, 13
Bassett, Thomas, deceased, 13
Bassett, Thomas, deceased, 14
Bates, Joseph, 17
Bates, Thomas, 23
Bay, Elihu Hall, 4
Bay, Elihu Hall, 4
Bay, Elihu Hall, 4
Bilbo, Matthew, deceased, 33
Biverest, Peter, 8
Blackwell, Nathan, 34
Boykin, Francis, 32
Brewer, George, Junior, 23
Brewer, George, Junior, 24
Brewer, George, Junior, 24
Brewer, John, 31
Brewer, John, 32
Broca, Du. See Dubroca

Broutin, Narciso, 9
Broutin, Narciso, 30
Bryant, Jesse, 35
Buford, William, 31
Burdon, George, 11
Burdon, George, 11
Burdon, George, 11
Burke, William, heirs of, 18
Burke, William, 32
Byrne, Gerald, 8
Callier, James, 35
Callier, James, 35
Campbell, Joseph, 30
Campbell, Joseph, 30
Campbell, Joseph, 35
Carpenter, Caleb, 15
Carpenter, Joseph, 15
Carpenter, Richard, 15
Carson, Thomas, 25
Castro, De. See De Castro
Chastang, Joseph, 26
Chastang, John, Doctor, 27
Chastang, John, Doctor, 27
Chastang, John, 27
Christmas, Natt, 17
Clark, William, 10
Cockaram, James, 35
Coleman, Francis, 5
Coleman, Francis, 5
Coleman, Richard, 29
Copelen, James, deceased, 23
Copelen, James, deceased, heirs of, 23
Daran, Francis, 7
Dawson, John, 6
De Olive, Dominique, 29
De Olive. See also Olive
De Castro, Julian, 35
Dean, Seth, 6
Dean, Seth, 6
Dean, Seth, 6
Deforge, Peter, 7
Deforge, Peter, heirs of, 10
Deforge, Peter, 10
Deforge, Peter, heirs of, 10
Deforge, Peter, 10

Demoy, Charles Arbon, 31
Denley, James, 15
Denley, James, 16
Denley, James, 16
Dubroca, Valentine, 24
Dupree, Howel, 22
Dyer, Reuben, 21
Epaho, Anthony, 3
Epaho. See also Aspaho
Espejo. See Aspaho; Epaho. (Translation for Mirror in Spanish)
Farmer, Robert, 1
Farmer, Robert, 1
Farr, James, 18
Fletcher, Josiah, 28
Forge, De. See Deforge
Foutinella, Francisco, 3
Fradgley, William, 4
Fradgley, William, 4
Fraser, James, 2
Frend, Samuel, 21
Friend. See Frend
Frouillet, Peter, heirs of, 3
Frouillet, Peter, 3
Gaines, Young, 17
Gains, Young, 2
Gains, Young, 9
Gillard, Theodore, 11
Gillard, Theodore, 11
Gillard, Theodore, 12
Gillard, Theodore, 12
Gillard, Theodore, 12
Grant, Alen, 11
Griffin, James, 24
Halverson. See Helverson
Harrison, Benjamin, 15
Hartly, Michael, 17
Hawkins, Richard, 17
Helverson, Godfrey, 22
Helverson, Godfrey, heirs of, 22
Henry, Lemuel, 26
Hillis, William, 22
Hinson, J., administrator, 23
Hoggatt, James, 5
Holinger, Adam, 20
Hollinger, Adam, 16

Hollinger, Adam, 32
Hooven, Benjamin, 18
Howard, Joshua, 5
Hunt, Abijah, 13
Hunt, William, 33
Jackson, William, 6
Johnson, Daniel, 22
Johnson, Daniel, 32
Johnson, John, 9
Johnson, John, 19
Johnson, Solomon, 16
Jones, Thomas, 18
Jurzan, Pitiagad, 9
Jurzan, Peter, 9
Juzan, Francis, 6
Killingworth, Francis, 25
King, Benjamin, 6
Lamb, Joseph, 11
Lawrence, Ann, 34
Lee, Richard, 33
Lewis, Francis, 12
Linder, John, Junior, 26
Linder, John, Senior, 26
Linder, John, Senior, 34
Little, Abraham, 5
Lott, John, Junior, 1
Lyons, Samuel, 35
Malone, Thomas, 9
Malone, Thomas, 29
McCullagh, Alexander, 1
McCullagh, Alexander, heirs of, 13
McCurtin, Cornelius, 2
McDaniel, William, 28
McGrew, Clarke, 35
McGrew, James, 18
McGrew, John F., 35
McIntosh, John, heirs of , 2
McIntosh, John, 2
Miller, Jacob, 15
Mills, James, 34
Mills, John, 25
Mills, William, 25
Milton, Michael, heirs of, 31
Milton, Michael, 31
Mims, Samuel, 2

Mims, Samuel, 7
Mims, Samuel, 10
Mims, Samuel, 20
Mirror. See Espejo (translation from Spanish)
Moore, Arthur, 5
Morgan, Jordan, 33
Morris, John, 8
Munger, Anna, 36
Munger, Hiram, 36
Munger, Sampson, 36
Narbone, Maria Josepia, 14
Olive, Dominique, 17
Olive, De. See De Olive
Perkins, N., 13
Perkins, Nicholas, 22
Perkins, Nicholas, 22
Perry, Hardy, 8
Phillips, George, 28
Phillips, Jeremiah, 31
Pierce, John, 31
Pierce, William, 31
Powell, William, heirs of, 7
Powell, William, 7
Powell, William, deceased, heirs of, 24
Powell, William, deceased, 24
Proctor, James, 20
Randon, John, 21
Rochan, Augustin heirs of, 4
Rochan, Augustin, 4
Rochan, Augustin, heirs of, 4
Rochan, Augstin, 4
Rochan, Austin, 13
Rochon, Augustine, deceased, heirs of, 14
Rochon, Augustine, deceased, 14
Rochon, Augustine, deceased, heirs of, 14
Rochon, Augustine, deceased, 14
Rochon, Augustine, 30
Rochon, Louisa, 30
Ryan, Isaac, 28
Scott, James, 34
Selhoof, Conrad, 31
Skipper, Michael, 19
Snelgrove, Henry, 35
Spiegel. See Epeho (German translation from Spanish)
Stedham, Moses, 20

Steel, Frances, 30
Stiggins, Joseph, 12
Stiggins, Joseph, 19
Stiggins, Joseph, 21
Sullivan, Owen, deceased, heirs of, 23
Sutherland, John, 4
Talley, John, 27
Thompson, Joseph, 19
Thompson, Joseph, 20
Trennier, John Baptiste, 28
Trennier, John Baptiste, 29
Turnbull, John, 2
Turnbull, John, 3
Turnbull, John, 8
Underwood, Thomas, 13
Vardeman, William, 1
Walker, Abraham, 25
Walker, Charles, 5
Walker, Charles, 6
Wall, William, 5
Ward, Charles, 12
Ward, Charles, 12
Ward, Daniel, 15
Watkins, James, 24
Webber, William, 32
Weekley, George, 19
Weekley, George, 19
Weekley, John, 18
Wheat, Thomas, 22
Wilks, Simeon, 20
Wooton, Hardy, 33

www.ingramcontent.com/pod-product-compliance
Lightning Source LLC
Chambersburg PA
CBHW081354230426
43667CB00017B/2832